People, Planet, Profit

People, Planet, Profit

How to embrace sustainability for innovation and business growth

Peter Fisk

KoganPage

LONDON PHILADELPHIA NEW DELHI

First published in Great Britain and the United States in 2010 by Kogan Page Limited

120 Pentonville Road	525 South 4th Street, #241	4737/23 Ansari Road
London N1 9JN	Philadelphia PA 19147	Daryaganj
United Kingdom	USA	New Delhi 110002
www.koganpage.com		India

© Peter Fisk, 2010

ISBN   978 0 7494 5411 1
E-ISBN   978 0 7494 5863 8

British Library Cataloguing-in-Publication Data

A CIP record for this book is available from the British Library.

Library of Congress Cataloging-in-Publication Data
Fisk, Peter (Peter Robert)
   People, planet, profit : how to embrace sustainability for innovation and business growth / Peter Fisk.
      p. cm.
   Includes index.
   ISBN 978-0-7494-5411-1 – ISBN 978-0-7494-5863-8   1.   Social responsibility of business. 2. Industrial management–Environmental aspects. 3. Corporations–Growth. 4. Social responsibility of business–Case studies. 5. Industrial management–Environmental aspects–Case studies. 6. Corporations–Growth–Case studies. I. Title.
   HD60.F535 2010
   658.4'083–dc22
                                                                                                2009048339

Typeset by Saxon Graphics Ltd, Derby
Printed and bound in Great Britain by MPG Books Ltd, Bodmin, Cornwall

For Anna and Clara

Contents

Introduction: People and Planet and Profit

We live in a time of unprecedented change.

In business we face challenges and opportunities that are more critical and complex than ever – where the consequences of failure are unimaginable and the impact of our decisions is felt instantly across the planet.

A fragile economy and a climate out of control, poverty across half the planet and scarcity of natural resources, the extinction of species and explosion in population, ethical dilemmas on every corner, and low confidence and trust in business: symptoms of a changing world.

Change is all around us: the cries for help at the end of an industrial age, the shift in power towards the developing world, from big to small, masses to niches, and the recognition that we can only sustain our livelihoods with new thinking, new behaviours and new balances.

We know that the old short-term, sales- and wealth-obsessed models of business are broken, and we are now beginning to feel the consequences. We struggle to balance our priorities and ambitions – the pursuit of personal and business success, whilst also seeking to make the world a better place. Is it possible to do both?

These are challenging times to lead and manage a business, even more difficult to create and sustain profitable growth.

Rethink

Social and environmental issues are more important than ever. For business, they represent some of the greatest opportunities to find new markets of profitable growth, more lasting and engaging sources of competitive advantage, and more effective ways to reduce cost and risk.

Consumers no longer feel conflicted by the issues, but are committed to supporting change. Doing good is no longer about sackcloth and frugality, it can feel and taste good too. We realize that it is no longer a nice-to-have, but a must-do. We realize that it is no longer a peripheral activity but fundamental to every aspect of how we do business, every day, for everyone.

People, Planet, Profit is about business opportunity, operational improvement and competitive advantage. It is a practical handbook for CEOs and business managers who are searching for new ways to create value, to make sense of business in a rapidly shifting landscape, to deliver profitable growth whilst also doing 'the right thing'. It is about:

- *Profitable growth:* finding new ways to sustain growth in a world that is changing rapidly, and can seem threatening and uncertain;
- *Innovation:* positively connecting capitalism and environmentalism, realigning issues and incentives, and making business a force for good;

- *Competitive advantage:* putting social and environmental impacts at the heart of your business, the basis of more engaging differentiation;
- *Leadership:* inspiring business to be the creators of this new world – to rethink, reframe and reinvent your business for a better future.

This is not really a book about sustainability in itself, about the world's problems, or about 'being green'. The last thing business needs is another dysfunctional strategy, more complex initiatives and distraction. Social and environmental issues should be at the core of a business strategy, leveraged as the best sources of improving efficiency and driving innovation, working with partners in new ways whilst also finding a more lasting difference, and a better way to engage people.

People, Planet, Profit is about inspiring leadership, more radical innovation and sustaining performance in the new business world.

Can business growth be good?

Of course, the world faces immense problems, so great that few organizations have the power or scale to solve them.

Business is unique in this sense. Through engaging brands and thoughtful innovation it can mobilize consumers to change behaviour in positive ways. By adapting the resources it uses and the ways it works, it can make a huge difference to the environment. It can be a powerful force of positive change.

There is no paradox or conflict, as some suggest. Business really can grow and be good.

People, planet and profit are not alternative goals, or a compromise result. A positive impact on people and planet can be achieved whilst also delivering profitable growth.

Indeed, a positive impact on people and planet is increasingly becoming the best source of profitable growth.

Despite a rapidly increasing global population and carbon emissions that threaten the air we breathe, it is possible to continue to grow economically and replenish the resources we use. Of course, it is likely to be a different sort of growth. It will be less about volume, more about profit; less materialistic production and more about supportive services, less self-indulgent and more about enabling people to live better lives.

Whilst the importance of social and environmental issues might seem obvious, they are not always seen as key to business success. Indeed, waves of restrictive legislation and anti-capitalist lobbying can put them in conflict. This is because we haven't seen the connections.

However, as Ben Clarke from Kraft Foods says, 'Sustainability is now about profit... it is the opportunity of the 21st century.'

The business case for people and planet and profit is based on both the profitable new opportunities of sustainable markets – embracing these issues within existing markets, and investing in new market spaces such as renewable energies – and also on the significant cost and risks likely to be incurred by unsustainable practices in future.

These growth opportunities are rapidly being embraced; the gold rush is on. Venture capitalists and entrepreneurs are now firmly focused on sustainable markets. Similarly the costs and risks are already hitting balance sheets. Investors are penalizing 'dirty' companies for their vulnerable future cash flows, and finance managers are calculating their liabilities.

The consequences of not changing are not just for the world we leave behind for our children, but more immediately through the liabilities of increasing financial penalties imposed by governments (for example, taxation on transport and industrial emissions), by supply chains, and ultimately by consumers (for example, the prohibitive cost of insurance in areas vulnerable to extreme weather).

Sustainability is no longer an adjunct to business. It is no longer a separate department, or even a team within the corporate affairs department concerned only about compliance and reputation. It is no longer enough to have some worthy goals, a sustainability strategy as an appendix to the business plan, or a sustainability report as an afterthought.

CSR (corporate social responsibility) strategies were typically peripheral compensation for the damages already done, relieving the guilt of companies that couldn't see the light. They were the clean, caring icing on the big dirty cake. They sought to protect superficial and increasingly fragile reputations.

'People and planet and profit' is much more than that. It is about moving the issues of sustainability from the fringes to the heart of business. It demands that business leaders rethink fundamental strategic questions: why we exist, where we should focus, how we are different, and why people will choose a product, want to work for us and invest in our business.

People and planet

The social and environmental challenges are known and numerous. But with rethinking they also represent some of the best opportunities for business.

Consider just some of them. As the global population mushrooms towards 9 million, cities like Beijing, Los Angeles and Mumbai will triple in size.

1950s – 60s **Awakening**	1970s – 80s **Regulating**	1990s – 00s **Contributing**	2010+ **Transforming**
• Industrial growth delivers wealth and expectation • Western markets thrive whilst the East recovers more slowly • Migration to cities accelerated by travel and employment • Flower-power hippies raise social and environment priorities	• Economic growth with increased consumerism and international trade • Product innovation supported by low-cost automated production • Improved lifestyles, human and equal rights lead to new practices • Government regulation on pollution and waste through taxation	• Multinational brands serve more diverse, informed and conscious customers • Digital innovation creates virtual businesses, faster and more connected • Corporate governance improves the ethical and social behaviour of business • Recycling, sustainable sourcing and disposal adopted as standard	• Global markets, with instant connectivity, global trends and rising 'base of the pyramid' • Sustainable innovation puts social and environmental issues at core of business • Collaborative organizations and networked communities for new business models • Sustainable markets are most profitable, as 'doing good' becomes the best way to grow

Figure 0.1 Sustainable agenda: how social and environmental issues have moved from the organization fringes to core business

Whilst the global middle class is the fastest growing section of society, with its high aspirations and higher consumption, a billion people survive on less than $1 a day, 3 billion on less than $2 a day.

Three billion people have no access to clean water, 800 million are hungry, and 10 million children die before they are five.

Yet those at the bottom of the pyramid have dreams too. They seek better lives and demand more. Together they represent an estimated $5 trillion market.

Add to this the environmental challenges. Every year we destroy 44 million acres of forest, creating an increasing imbalance in the way nature produces and absorbs carbon dioxide. We lose 100 million acres of farmland, cutting down trees, diverting natural irrigation and creating 15 million acres of new desert around the world. We emit 8 billion tonnes of carbon into our atmosphere, only 3 billion tonnes of which can be reabsorbed. We use 160 billion

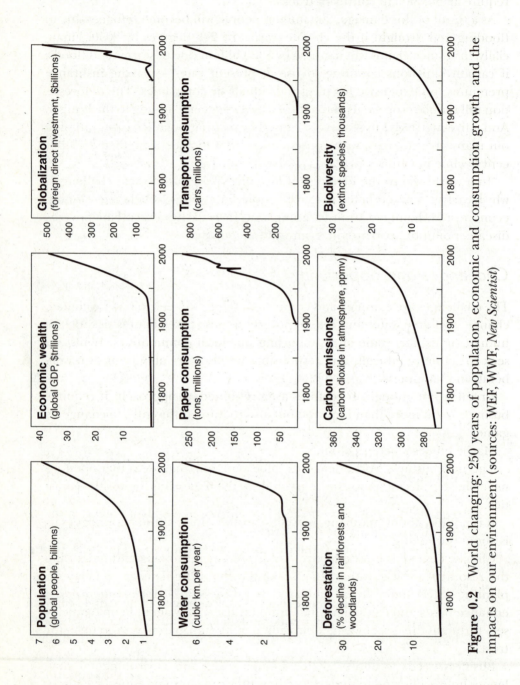

Figure 0.2 World changing: 250 years of population, economic and consumption growth, and the impacts on our environment (sources: WEF, WWF, *New Scientist*)

tons more water each year than is being replenished by rain, enough to require a 450,000 km convoy of trucks.

As a result of this damage, 200 million people will become refugees due to flooding and drought if the climate warms by 2–3 degrees by 2050. Financially, insurance claims will increase by $320 billion due to storms and floods, if carbon emissions continue to rise at present rates – making insurance premiums too expensive for most individuals or companies. The deforestation will reduce crop yields across Africa by 33 per cent, adding to the hunger. And a five-metre rise in sea levels, caused by melting polar ice caps, will wipe out many coastal areas, with consequences that include a predicted 11 per cent decline in China's GDP.

'In a world where the ideology of free enterprise has no real challenges, why have free markets failed so many people?' questions Nobel Prize-winning economist Muhammad Yunus, arguing that 'Instead they exacerbate poverty, disease, pollution, corruption, crime and inequality.'

Challenges and opportunity

The challenges are complex and connected. Whilst we seek to reverse climate change, conserve water and relieve poverty, we also care about issues such as human rights, fair trade and supporting our local communities. Whilst we seek to act more ethically and responsibly, we also care about our own well-being and happiness.

Green is not enough. It requires a more joined-up approach. It requires business to do more than improve, but also to think differently, to change its game.

Maybe blue is a better colour.

The new business world demands 'blue sky' thinking, ideas that open up new 'blue oceans' of opportunity and redraw the blueprints for business practice.

It is not just about 'reducing, recycling and reusing', as the mantra goes. It is about rethinking.

Climate change is most effectively addressed by rethinking and redefining the resources we use, rather than seeking to limit the damage by belatedly planting a few more trees. Similarly, in business it is not about product enhancements and campaigns that jump on the bandwagon. People quickly see through the greenwash, demanding real transparency in return for trust.

Business needs to address its economic, social and environmental challenges holistically, and to understand how they can combine as positive forces in creating a better world.

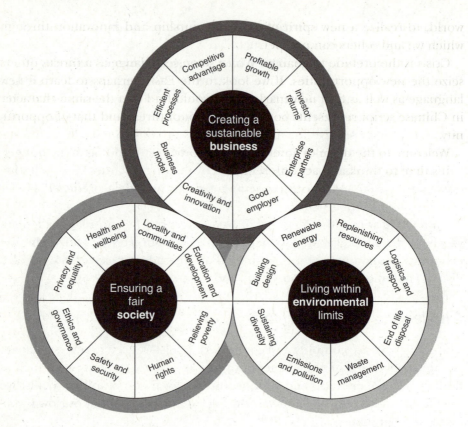

Figure 0.3 People and planet and profit: economic growth is only sustainable if business activities are integrated with social and environmental priorities (source: Genius Works)

'People and planet and profit' is a more connected approach to business. It demands systems thinking, seeing the bigger picture of why and how we work. It will require us to reject many of the conventions and conveniences of business that created past success; taking new perspectives, finding new solutions, and even finding new measures of performance.

It requires us to reconnect with consumers who have lost faith, suppliers who feel beaten up, and sometimes even with competitors where together we can have more impact.

Inspired leaders

It demands the vision and courage of business leaders, and every manager across the organization, to release business from the shadows of a failing world, to realize a new spirit of entrepreneurship and innovation through which we and others can prosper.

Crisis is the prelude to change. Whilst some see change as a threat, others seize the new opportunities. If we look to the East, perhaps to learn a new language as well as find new markets, we would find that the same character in Chinese script represents both the concept of threat and that of opportunity.

Welcome to the dawn of a new business world.

It's time to think and act differently.

The People, Planet, Profit Manifesto

Leaders of business, this is your wake-up call.
You've been living on borrowed time.

Raping the natural world of its resources, and leaving a toxic mess in its place.
These weather patterns are not freaks, they are the world you have created.

Blinding the man on the street with your superficial innovations and image.
What about the sweatshops, the emissions, the packaging, the greed?

It doesn't look good.

Business, society and nature need to find a new way to coexist.
If you aren't sustainable, you are irresponsible.

It's time to adapt or suffer the consequences.

The business world is about to go through a rapid, fundamental change.
What an opportunity, but also what a threat.

It's time to rethink.

Time to stop living in the past, and think of our future.
Business is not a machine, it's a dynamic system – it lives, adapts and grows.

You need to think again about what is a cost and a risk, and what really creates value in the world today.

But it will take a lot more than reducing, recycling and reusing.
It requires a fundamental rethink, radically and creatively.

Rethink your business purpose and strategy.
Rethink your processes and technologies.
Rethink your markets and audiences.

Imagine that you are looking at a piece of impressionist art. Short term, too close, you are blinded by millions of dots; stand back and you see a bigger vision.

The environment is not a commodity, and people are not disposable.

New legal codes and financial penalties will protect them.

But this is not just about compliance. It's much more than CSR.
It goes to the heart of business. To why you exist.
Where you focus, how you succeed.
To connect business and the world in new ways.

People and planet and profit. Together, achieving more.

Business is a societal good. It has a responsibility beyond itself.
Brands and consumerism, profits and wealth can be incentives for change.
Available to anyone, the benefits shared by everyone.

Be brave. Seek out ideas beyond your comfort zone.

Create a new language of sustainability that transcends traditional disciplines.
Redefine stakeholders more broadly.

Everything is possible. Nothing is off limits.
From nuclear energy to GM foods, we need to rethink our prejudices too.

Collaborate with your competitors, and even your fiercest critics.
Work with governments and activists to explore new solutions.

Together we can do so much more.

We need innovation to find new ways to overcome conflicting priorities, to make inspired choices, to find brilliant new balances.

Sustainability is about creating a more lasting and fairer world.
Where we can work and play, laugh and smile.

And our children will be able to too.

Grow by putting our future at the heart of your business.
Grow better by being and doing good as a business.

Be bold and brilliant.

Be the change.

Part 1

Rethinking business

'Be the change,' said Mahatma Gandhi.

My world: Kris, the Indian computer engineer

Kris is 34, married with three children, and works for one of the world's fastest-growing technology companies, based in the Indian high-tech metropolis of Bangalore. He previously studied for an engineering degree in London and MBA in Boston.

He recognizes that he has done well in an emerging country of many extremes – religion and history, poverty and wealth. 'India has one of the fastest-growing middle classes, where families like mine have many of the trappings of Western lifestyle. We have satellite TV and a 4×4 Toyota car. We go to the cinema, and next year hope to take our children to Disneyland.'

But he has not lost touch with the masses of Indians who still live in relative poverty, with few material goods and limited ambitions in life. 'My parents, my two brothers and both of their families all live in a small house near to Mumbai. They earn little money, working in factories and in construction. Their need to earn money has meant they have never trained for any specific job, and what I find saddest is that they have limited ambition. They live for today.'

Kris is increasingly aware of the social and environmental challenges his country faces. Whilst the Asian tsunami of 2005 dramatically raised awareness of the perils of a changing climate, he is much more concerned about improving the quality of life of his fellow citizens. 'We need to sort out the most urgent issues first, the ones that directly affect people.'

He spends some time doing voluntary work with his children's school, but thinks that he can make a bigger difference by encouraging his business to do more for local communities – supporting local charities, encouraging local businesses and using the skills and solutions of his employees for non-profit initiatives, as well as for their core business purpose.

'Whilst the world is more joined up, I think we are still very different. As Indian companies become respected for their quality and innovation I see the opportunity to do much more. Not just to become wealthy, but to use our know-how to support our country in solving its problems, and to improve the lives of everyone. I see business, and particularly high technology companies, as very important in creating a better future for my family and my country.'

My world: Claire the South African banker

Claire is 22 and lives in Soweto, South Africa with her parents and siblings. She's a bank clerk and student.

On sustainable living she says: 'We have our own vegetable garden in the yard, we use leftover food and produce waste as compost. And on fertile soil, we don't even have to buy seeds for our tomatoes and potatoes to grow. The quality is great and at least we know what went into the process, also fewer plastic (shopping) bags…'

When asked about her motivation, Claire reflects, 'I guess we started living green since I was a kid, My mom has always been passionate about planting her own food, so we've always eaten tomatoes, spinach, pumpkin and potatoes from the front-yard garden… We've only ever walked to go buy produce from the guy on the street corner, we water our garden with bath water.'

On trade-offs Claire says: 'My lifestyle is very simple, so I haven't as yet sacrificed much. I don't even drive, I like carrying my shopping bags and eating the freshest veggies. Where's the inconvenience there?'

She does wish the authorities would do something to help encourage recycling paper and bottles: 'I am currently unable to do so as we do not have any recycling bins to separate the stuff … I feel real guilty throwing paper into the bin with everything else … and Soweto is a very big part of Gauteng, most of Johannesburg's population lives there … and consume a whole lot.'

In terms of improving things, Claire believes a little education can go a long way: 'One community is given a quick lesson on how to start and sustain a vegetable garden, and they can then teach their neighbours. Educating the little kids about the importance of separating the trash would be a good start as well, I mean if every Friday there was a bottle and paper collecting van that went around the area … Starting small is the way to go, and I don't think the government is being innovative enough.

'Hell, I've never even seen Al Gore's movie about saving the planet. How aware am I really? Take it to the masses, because, honestly, all this recycling stuff has been glamorized and makes the ordinary man feel like he cannot contribute much … and that's because private individuals are pushing the cause more than government.'

My world: Grant, the American entrepreneur

Thirty-seven-year-old entrepreneur Grant lives in Wilton, Connecticut with his wife and two young children. He is the founder of FirstRide, with its mission statement 'Do good, do well', an interactive group that generates ideas to make it easier for people to make greener choices.

GreenerMags.com is a digital magazine platform and FirstRide Cars ('safer, cooler, greener cars') was started to provide a web service through which consumers could order a hybrid car at a flat price. The original aim of this initiative was to promote greener driving, not to make a profit.

He takes his business values further by working from home and getting together with his colleagues once a week: 'I live in Connecticut and my studio was in Brooklyn. I recently gave up my studio to work from home so I wouldn't have to commute. I miss the energy of Brooklyn, but go in once a week now instead of every day. It makes me feel good not to commute.'

Grant believes in making a difference 'by sharing good ideas and adopting a greener approach to living, by trying to get better every day'. He sees the role of green business as one of active involvement on many levels – 'alternative energy, organic food, hybrid/electric cars, recycling, recycled products, corp-orate-policy consulting firms' – and has built his business on the model 'PPP: people, planet, profit'.

He drives a Honda Civic hybrid, a purchase that was motivated by his busi-ness, uses energy-saving light bulbs, and recycles. He admits to using too much water ('Got to wash the kids and water the garden!'), says he'd like to get into composting ('but haven't made enough effort') and would like to video confer-ence instead of travelling for business ('but clients are not willing to change their practice').

1 Purpose beyond profits

- How to find the difference you make to the world.
- How to articulate this as a business vision and brand promise.
- How to align your organization in order to turn promises into reality.

Successful business is about more than money.

As the late great Anita Roddick, founder of Body Shop, once said, ethical and environmental convictions can drive businesses rather than hold them back. 'I want to work for a company that contributes to and is part of the community. I want something not just to invest in. I want something to believe in.'

Business should make a difference to the world in which we live – improving people's lives and improving physical and social habitats. If this can be supported with an appropriate business model, then making a difference can become a more sustainable source of profitable growth. If business fails to make our lives better in some way – physically or emotionally, instantly or eventually – then it is likely to be revealed as a commodity of little value, and find itself in a constant fight for survival.

Missions and visions, brand definitions and slogans dominate the mantras of most organizations. Yet most of these directional statements are superficial and short-sighted. They seek to make money without giving anything back... 'to create the best products' or 'to be the first choice' or 'to maximize returns to shareholders'.

The long view

Business becomes short term because it does not see a long term any different from today. It is typically unable to make sense of the most significant changes happening all around us, and therefore unwilling to act now to secure advantage in a changing world.

Managing a business with a higher purpose is like committing to a better way of life. Sustainability is like a lifestyle change – to eat more healthily, to keep fit, to explore the world. By adapting your outlook, you see and seize new opportunities.

These challenges take time and patience, discipline and perseverance. Consider the success of Google based on their purpose: to organize the world's information. They continually innovate towards this goal, whilst retaining flexibility to respond to a changing world. Their market value is based more on this intent rather than short-term results.

A purpose beyond profit is about defining how the business ultimately adds value to society. Indeed, what business calls 'sustainability' is not a goal in itself, but a means to get somewhere better. It is a how rather than a why. A purpose is energizing. It gives us cause and focus, and gives people a reason to love us.

As Virgin entrepreneur Sir Richard Branson said recently, his guiding principle in creating a business is 'to make a difference', and his personal test of this is 'Would people miss us if we were not around?'

Making people's lives better

Most businesses develop a mission statement about being the best they can be. However, these goals are usually introverted and self-serving. They are about being the best company in their sector, developing the highest-quality products or making the most money.

Whilst these objectives might indeed be important, they are worthless without a higher purpose. Strategies give companies direction and priorities, and leaders help motivate people to work with focus and pace, but there is something more to creating a business in which people thrive, where there is an energy, where people jump out of bed and turn up with a bounce and a thirst to do a great job.

Business ultimately exists to make a difference – a difference economically by creating value, in that it takes an investment and uses it to create something worthwhile, which people are prepared to pay for, and if the economics work out, then the business delivers a profit, which can then be shared as deemed appropriate by the many internal and external stakeholders. Investors get a return on their investment, employees get a return on their efforts, and customers get a return on their loyalty through investment in better solutions over time.

Now and forever

Whilst some companies and their shareholders can become blinkered by the pursuit of a quick buck – short-term greed – most realize that they need to give investments time to sink in, develop better products, enter better markets, build stronger brand reputations, before they can see the rewards.

The question therefore is not really about shareholder greed, but about the purpose of a business beyond making money. If it doesn't have such a purpose, it appears greedy.

If there is a genuinely good and compelling reason why the organization exists beyond making money, then everyone stops seeking to optimize the existing revenue streams, and commits to a higher purpose. Yes they still seek a return, but in a bigger context. Whilst there are many excellent not-for-profit businesses that support good causes, for-profit businesses can do so much more for the world too, and still grow profitably.

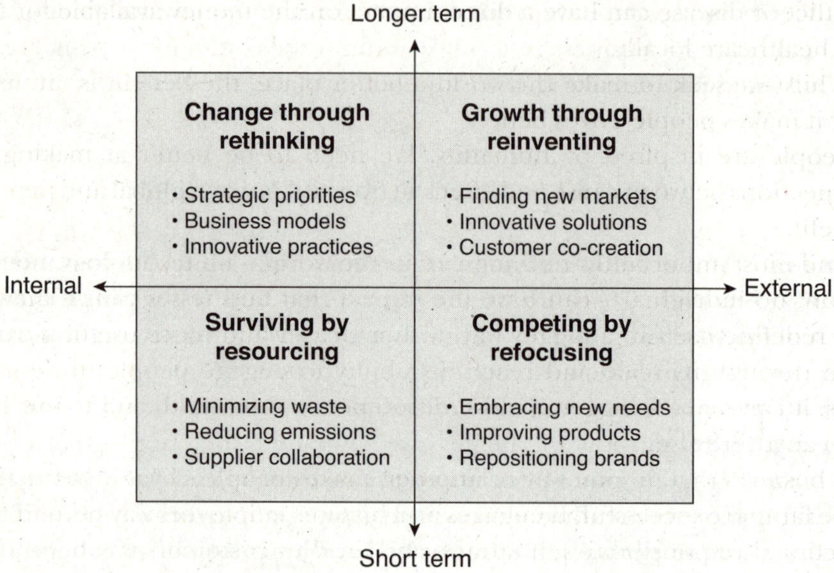
Longer term
Change through rethinking
• Strategic priorities
• Business models
• Innovative practices
Growth through reinventing
• Finding new markets
• Innovative solutions
• Customer co-creation
Internal
External
Surviving by resourcing
• Minimizing waste
• Reducing emissions
• Supplier collaboration
Competing by refocusing
• Embracing new needs
• Improving products
• Repositioning brands
Short term

Figure 1.1 Short and longer term: finding a better balance in the pursuit of sustained profitable growth

Making lives better

Ultimately a business is about making people's lives better. Of course, there are many ways to achieve this – it could mean functionally better by improving their health and wellbeing, to achieve things more easily or cheaply, to work faster or more effectively, or emotionally better by meeting new people, exploring new places, enjoying life more, or simply by putting a smile on their faces.

The impact might be direct or indirect – making the world we live in a better place – by addressing the malaise of poverty in faraway lands, reducing the impact of waste and emissions on the planet's ecology, supporting important medical or scientific research, or by supporting orphaned children in distant or local communities.

In a connected and interdependent world, these more indirect actions might feel remote, but increasingly they have a direct impact on our own livelihoods. Charitable aid or voluntary work might seem like a one-way donation, but done right, they are an investment in our own world.

Deforestation in South America has a direct climatic impact on the weather patterns of northern Europe. Supporting social entrepreneurs in India can make a direct impact on innovations available in North America. Reducing conflict or disease can have a direct impact on the money available for positive healthcare locally.

Whilst we seek to make the world a better place, the benefit is ultimately that it makes people's lives better.

People are inspired by humanity. We need to be better at making the connections between cause and effect, action and impact, global and personal benefit.

And most importantly, nothing else in the world – no technology, no institution, no individual – can have the impact that businesses can. If business can redefine itself in a bigger way, with a clearer and more useful purpose, then through its scale and reach, its ability to engage people in desirable ways, it can make a bigger positive difference to our world, and to our lives, than anything else.

A business that, in one way or another, makes people's lives better is likely to be far more successful. It engages and inspires employees way beyond their functional responsibilities, it attracts and enables customers way beyond the products and services they buy. It rewards shareholders, governments and communities in ways well beyond its economic outputs.

One way to think about this is Richard Branson's question: 'Would people miss you if you weren't around?' Another is to think how big a difference you could really make to people.

Defining an inspiring purpose

John Mackey, CEO of Whole Foods Markets, believes that businesses will only succeed in future if they realize that a business has to pursue a deeper purpose beyond shareholder value. 'People want businesses to do good in the world. It's that simple,' he proclaims.

The founder of the fresh and organic food business says, 'I believe that most of the greatest companies in the world also have great purposes that were discovered or created by their original founders and that still remain at the core of their business models. Having a deeper, more transcendent purpose is highly energizing for all of the various interdependent stakeholders, including the customers, employees, investors, suppliers, and the larger communities in which the business participates.'

Back in 1980 his first store in Austin, Texas set out with an inspired purpose: to help everyone live a more natural and healthy life. Mackey and his team capture this in their mantra, 'Whole Foods, Whole People, Whole Planet', with all three components being core to their approach.

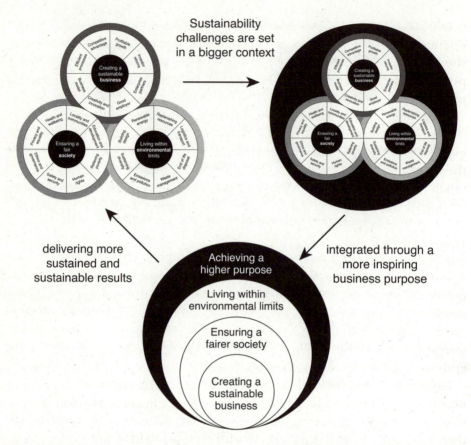

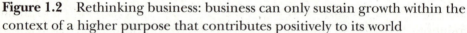

Figure 1.2 Rethinking business: business can only sustain growth within the context of a higher purpose that contributes positively to its world

Making business matter

A business purpose should be important, relevant and inspiring.

It should be significant in the impact it can have on society, but also a significant stretch in that it is difficult to achieve. It should be important in that it matters to people, either practically or emotionally, and might address a serious problem locally or globally, or it might be something less serious but nevertheless enhances people's lives.

A business purpose should be simple, distinctive and memorable.

It should capture the distinctive character and role of the organization well beyond the products and services it makes, but it should also guide which products and services it does offer. It should benefit more people than the immediate customers, but it should also be meaningful to those customers.

A business purpose should live inside and outside the business.

It should guide business strategy, from the markets in which you seek to operate, though to the criteria for decision making and prioritization. It should influence why and how people work, their attitudes and behaviours, performance and rewards. But it should be mostly about customers, and this motivates employees too.

A business purpose becomes transparent, natural and intuitive.

It is much more than a mission statement, although it might well be expressed in one line. It is also much more than a brand definition, although the brand should be the creative interpretation of the purpose. It is certainly much more than an advertising slogan. It's not about generic sets of values, or clever phrases. It's real. It's living. It's what you do, and why.

Brands and consumers

Tom Chappell is the co-founder of Tom's of Maine, which produces natural personal-care products without any chemicals or artificial ingredients. His products are kosher and halal as they contain no animal ingredients. They are cruelty free, good for vegans, and 10 per cent of pre-tax profits go to more worthy organizations. They are also some of the best products on the market, endorsed by doctors and dentists.

Tom's shows that ethical and environmental considerations can drive business – not as derivative benefits, but sitting at the heart of why you do business. 'At the heart of our story and the growth of Tom's of Maine is the fact that, now as then, the work begins with a set of beliefs and values. Those beliefs and values guide us every day in how we create products and build relationships. Something in us wants to endure beyond retained earnings. That something is our soul.'

A corporate brand, or a 'monolithic' architecture of product brands that supports a core brand, is perhaps the best platform through which to convey the purpose.

Brands at their heart are organizing ideas, which are then articulated in words and designs, colours and slogans, behaviours and environments. However, many brands still have the wrong idea that they are describing the business or product. Brands are about their audiences, and what they do for them, reflecting their needs and aspirations, and expressed as benefits, not features. Other stakeholders – employees, investors, partners, and broader society – matter too, but they are most motivated by what the brand does for customers.

However, when a business purpose is defined in a more sustainable context – with relevance to how the business adds value to society and environment

– then it is easy for the benefit to seem remote and abstract. This is why social issues are more engaging than environmental ones, and why making lives better is more compelling than making the world better. Your challenge is to emotionally connect with people at a higher level.

The purpose therefore is developed based on a framework of three components: rationally, what you do for people that makes their lives better; comparatively, how this is better than could be achieved otherwise; and emotionally, how people feel as a result. The purpose is expressed as an amalgam of these three components. And everything else the business does then follows.

Turning promises into reality

It is one thing to define a purpose, and turn it into a superbly admired and compelling promise to customers, but quite another thing to deliver it.

The implications of 'being good' as a business must have coherence in everything you do – from the style of advertising (and the sustainable media you use) to the product delivery (and its hopefully limited packaging), from the style of service (the awareness and thoughtful behaviour of people) through to support and relationships (you care, you try to do more). And of course it has implications for the suppliers you choose and how you treat them, the people you recruit and how you reward them, the partners you choose to work with.

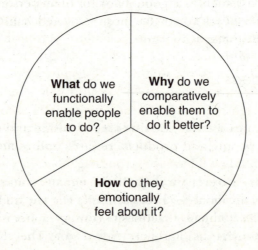

Figure 1.3   Higher purpose: business purpose has three components: functional, comparative and emotional (source: Genius Works)

The Co-operative Bank, for example, is a relatively small bank with its origins in the industrial communities of the North West of England. It was trusted by everyday people who preferred to support a local bank rather than a global giant. But it also needed to compete, and so in recent years looked to its heritage and its strengths to find what made it different from the likes of Barclays and HSBC.

It defined itself as 'the ethical bank' and went to great lengths to ensure that it was good. It carefully audited potential investments, to avoid supporting questionable industries or regimes. It also did much to support environmental issues, from coating its head office in solar panels to recycling the cooking oils from staff restaurants as fuel for its company vehicles.

Customers appreciated this, but it still didn't make a big difference to their own lives. The ethical approach needed to be more personal and tangible. Rather than just developing a 'good' halo, the bank started to reinvent products that enabled people to support good causes every time they used their credit card, insurance or investment. It rediscovered its caring, communal nature. It became more open and transparent, developing policy structures guided by customers, and rethinking how it could deliver service that is really wanted by and useful to people.

Most importantly, as the banking system collapsed around the world, customers saw this bank as responsible, not just for society, but for people and their money too. It was trusted.

The Co-operative Bank is now recognized as a leader in its sustainable practices, but also by customers as a 'good' bank for them personally as well as for the world. In 2008 it was voted the most respected bank in the UK, and number one for customer satisfaction.

Organizing ideas

The purpose therefore becomes an 'organizing idea'. More than strategy, it defines and shapes the way you do things – inside and out, culture and communication, people and products, rewards and relationships, service and style.

However, people care even more about the fair and consistent delivery of a promise than they do about the promise itself. The fair trade- and community-supporting coffee company that doesn't conserve water is inconsistent and punished by customers, as Starbucks found out. The carefully designed household recycling schemes by local councils are welcomed, until their carbon-emitting collection vehicles clog up the streets and do more perceived harm than good.

Even the company that promises 'the real thing' has realized that it needs to do more, to ensure that that promise becomes a reality. With increasing awareness of water as a scarce resource, and of health as a global priority, The Coca-Cola Company has no choice but to think differently.

Coke's CEO, Mehmet Kant, argues that 'a sustainable business relies on the sustainability of the communities and businesses [that] it operates in. We recognize that we need to be part of the solution on global issues that threaten the communities we serve, and that are relevant to our business.'

Brand owners realize that all they really have is their reputations, and that even the most powerful brands are fragile in today's world. Strength is not in the sexiness of an image, the catchiness of advertising or the amount spent on it. Brands live and die in the minds of their audiences, yet if they have an inspiring purpose, they have more chance of mattering more to people, doing more for people, and living longer.

Google and Microsoft: finding purpose in a digital world

Microsoft's founder Bill Gates famously defined as his purpose, 'to put a computer in every home and on every desk', whilst his arch rivals Sergey Brin and Larry Page at Google slightly more recently described their purpose as to 'organize the world's information'.

Google and Microsoft have much in common. Both are US-based companies with global reach, offering computer software (and increasingly hardware too) that helps businesses and individuals to live more fulfilling, informed and productive lives (the real benefit of their rather productized own definitions).

Their direct environmental impacts are relatively light, since their products do not require armies of staff and huge manufacturing operations to produce.

More importantly, both companies wield huge influence in the day-to-day lives of billions of people across the globe, dictating much of how they live, work and learn. Of particular concern to consumers and activists, for example, are how user data are stored and used and how information is delivered to (or held back from) users of their search engines.

Google's challenge

According to Sergey Brin, 'Some say Google is God, others say Google is Satan.' Google's adopted mantra, 'Don't be evil,' sets out its position on the matter.

With total assets of more than $25 billion, almost as many users as there are people with access to the internet, and terabytes of data on the surfing habits of these users, there is no doubting Google's power and influence in almost every walk of life.

Google, claims Brin, is very much about making money, but it also aspires to be 'innovative, trusted and ethical'. Indeed, the way in which Google conducts its business is perceived to be key to its success.

Google's tens of thousands of employees appreciate their relaxed working environment, with its emphasis on casual dress and having fun in a productive environment; Google topped Forbes Magazine's list of 100 Best Places to Work in both 2007 and 2008. Google's philosophy places emphasis on values such as 'You can be serious without a suit,' and 'Work should be challenging and the challenge should be fun.'

Perhaps inevitably, given its size and influence, Google has found itself at the centre of several controversies related to its business practices and services. For example, it has been accused of complicity in the attempts of the governments of China, France and Germany to filter search results in accordance with regional laws and regulations, and privacy campaigners accuse it of storing personal information for longer than necessary.

Some governments have expressed nervousness over the security implications of Google Earth, a tool that allows users to access sky photographs of geographical locations around the world. Google has also been criticized by advertisers for allegedly failing to combat click fraud, which can increase the cost to its advertising clients.

As has been mentioned, the CO_2 emissions of Google's operations are light when compared with other industries. However, considerable amounts of energy are required to power the millions of servers, computers, monitors and cooling units needed to deliver Google's services to end users.

Google's response

Google's sustainability investments fall into two main areas: human well-being (especially for its own staff) and energy efficiency (to reduce both greenhouse gas emissions and energy bills). For its staff, Google provides free organic food in its 'Googleplex' canteen, subsidizes the purchase of energy-efficient vehicles, and sponsors a Google Environmental Fair, at which staff members can learn about sustainable products, lifestyles and working practices.

Google seeks to reduce its environmental impacts by running its US headquarters entirely on solar power, of which plenty is available in its home state of California. Google also lobbies its peers in the IT industry to improve the energy efficiency of their hardware, which has the added benefit of saving Google millions of dollars in energy bills for cooling its servers. Google also helps to fund carbon-reduction projects in Asia, via the UN's Clean Development Mechanism (a part of the Kyoto Protocol).

Google recently announced plans to invest $500 million in a new initiative to develop sources of renewable energy that can undercut the costs of conventional power. As part of this initiative – with the catchy title of 'Renewable Energy Cheaper Than Coal' – Google plans to buy companies and hire engineers to develop new and more affordable solar, geothermal, wind and other alternative energy sources. Google expects to achieve this goal within 'years, not decades'.

Microsoft's challenge

From Windows to Xbox, Microsoft is a dominant player in the manufacture of both software and processors for personal and business computing.

The majority of Microsoft's products, especially software, have relatively minor 'direct' impacts, but the way in which they are designed has major impacts on the energy consumption and design of computers, servers and other IT equipment.

For example, well-designed software can reduce the amount of energy required by computer processing units (CPUs); computer hardware, including PCs and MP3 players, can be designed to allow software upgrades and the modification of components, rather than being thrown away when the next model comes to market.

Perhaps most significantly, Microsoft's products act as tools for businesses and individuals to carry out their daily tasks more efficiently and effectively. For example, the development of e-mail, video conferencing and other communications software reduces the amount of physical mail that needs to be transported by road, rail and air, with its associated demands on material and energy resources; and computer-aided design (CAD) applications help designers and planners devise more efficient manufacturing, public transport and urban systems.

The United States alone generates more than 2 million tonnes of e-waste per year, much of which is exported to developing countries for disassembly, often in poorly regulated environments. If handled responsibly, obsolete computer hardware can be reused, recycled and safely decommissioned; irresponsible decommissioning, on the other hand, can pose health risks to humans, release litter and harmful toxins into the environment, and waste precious resources (such as rare metals).

The challenge for Microsoft, therefore, is to develop products and services that minimize the use of electricity and materials that remain in use for longer periods of time, that help people and businesses to work more efficiently, and that are responsibly decommissioned.

Microsoft's response

Microsoft has begun to make significant advances in both the energy intensity of its products and the efficiency of production.

At a corporate level, Microsoft has provided the Clinton Foundation with online software that enables cities around the world to monitor and measure their carbon emissions. It has operated a bus commuter service for its Seattle-based employees, and constructed a data centre near Quincy, Washington to take advantage of a nearby source of hydroelectric renewable energy. And it announced a partnership with WhatOnEarthsGoingOn.com to enable internet users to support charitable causes.

At a product level, Microsoft has incorporated improved energy-management features in its Windows Vista operating system, superior to those found in the older Windows XP; and it has reduced the energy demands of its Windows Server 2008 system by 20 per cent when compared with previous Windows server systems.

In 2000, Bill and Melinda Gates established a charitable foundation to support initiatives that improve health, promote free public access to digital information and fight poverty. In 2007 alone, the Bill and Melinda Gates Foundation Trust distributed grants worth a staggering $2 billion.

The impact

Google's focus on staff wellbeing, innovation and energy efficiency should bring dividends not only for the company and its shareholders, but also for the environment: happier staff tend to be more productive; cheaper, cleaner sources of energy will not only cut costs for Google and its peers in the IT industry but also make a significant contribution to mitigating climate change. It remains to be seen whether or not these efficiency gains will be swamped by the explosive growth of the IT industry, which is currently responsible for approximately 2 per cent of global carbon emissions.

Microsoft has initiated a number of actions to reduce the environmental impacts of its facilities and products, most notably with relation to energy sourcing and efficiency. However, Microsoft's biggest contribution to sustainability has come through the Bill and Melinda Gates Foundation Trust, a charitable body that is not part of Microsoft Corporation. Some see this independence as an advantage, providing greater scope and flexibility for philanthropic activities on an unprecedented scale. Others believe that it lets Microsoft Corporation off the hook when it comes to aligning its core activities with environmental and social concerns.

The breadth and complexity of Microsoft's own operations and product lines call for a more strategic and coordinated approach to sustainability, based on an understanding not only of its own operations, but of how its products and services are used by customers and consumers. For example, Microsoft has failed substantially to address the problem of obsolescence, whereby customers are encouraged to replace hardware that is still in good working order. Indeed, many of the environmental improvements that Microsoft has developed, such as the improved energy efficiency of its Windows operating and server systems, are available only to purchasers of new equipment.

People, planet, profit: the reality of purpose

How Unilever are building brands with a conscience

'The 21st century is a time of scarcity in terms of natural resources,' argues Santiago Gowland, director of sustainability. 'The 20th century was all about abundance, and business externalities were not too important as long as wealth was created. Now, wealth creation must considered more holistically.'

Business people, he believes, have changed in outlook, and want to work with more purpose.

'People don't want to work until they are 60 or 70 and focus only on wealth to retire and drop some coins into a charity to feel they are doing good. Talented professionals today want to integrate their values into their professions and contribute to becoming part of the solution to some of the issues they see every day in the newspapers. They want to bring the whole of themselves to work and in doing that, they unleash the power of their imagination that is connected to heart affections, to values, to their own search for meaning.'

Brands allow us to extend the conversation with consumers, moving from functional to emotional and social issues. Look at Dove, Ben & Jerry's, Lipton, Lifebuoy. These are just four Unilever brands that are moving beyond the limited world of consumer individual needs to engage in a broader conversation about that consumer's shared world (community) and even about some of the biggest challenges that 'the world' is facing. This is only possible due to the existence of brands.

'That's where Naomi Klein's book fails,' argues the passionate Argentinian. 'Brands are becoming the biggest lever to transforming the business agenda in a profitable way.'

We are living in the end of abundance era. And whilst we go from 6 to 9 billion people – all aspiring to live better – these social, economic and environmental challenges continue to grow. The question of the role of business in society and the concept of economic growth as we traditionally understand them need to be revised.

The evidence is readily articulated. 'Health epidemics and infectious diseases are also on the rise,' says Gowland. 'The world's biggest killers are AIDS, TB and malaria. A child dies every 30 seconds from malaria and pregnant women are particularly vulnerable. More than 12 million children in sub-Saharan Africa have been orphaned by AIDS – set to rise to 43 million by 2010.

'People living in poverty are disproportionably vulnerable to disease. Fifteen million children die from malnutrition each year. That's one person every 3.6 seconds. The gap between rich and poor continues to grow. As everyone knows, 20 per cent of the world has 80 per cent of the wealth and that wealth is concentrated in the developed parts of the world. Half the world's assets are held by two per cent of the population. Or, to put it another way, half the world's population own one per cent of its assets.

'One billion people lack access to safe drinking water and 2.5 billion people – half the developing world – lack access to basic sanitation. Unclean water is a primary cause of diarrhoea, the world's second-biggest killer of children. Climate change is now a reality and a growing threat. This century is witnessing the end to abundance. Scarcity is the rule. Growing populations and rising affluence are putting food, energy and water resources under stress.'

Purpose has to come before profit, he proclaims. 'Stating that there is one and only one social responsibility in business – to use its resources and engage in activities designed to increase its profits so long as [this] stays within the rules of the game, which is to say, [engaging] in open and free competition without deception or fraud – is unacceptable, not only by [21st-century] society but even by business leaders who are trying to find a new articulation to the role of business that will improve Friedman's concept.'

Unilever knows it cannot change the world, but can make a real difference. 'Companies cannot transform the world on their own but as has been expressed in the Johannesburg declaration, they have a role to play, starting with transforming themselves. We cannot continue trying to justify every value or moral consideration with the articulation of a business case.'

Why the WWF is redefining the value drivers

The Worldwide Fund for Nature (WWF) has very long had engagement with business, seeing this collaboration as an essential way to effect change in the natural world. But the agenda is changing rapidly. The environment has become an important social agenda, and brands like Body Shop have moved from niche to mainstream.

David Nussbaum, WWF chief executive, believes that 'Many businesses have recognized that their own operations face environmental challenges to their own sustainability, and that their access to the best staff and the commitment and loyalty of the best staff depends not only on them being excellent operationally and commercially, but also done in a way that echoes their changing personal values.'

He gives the changing nature of asset values – from house price to corporation valuations – as an example of the impact of this changing agenda. 'House prices are more influenced by how much energy people are going to spend to heat [the house],' and similarly market capitalizations increasingly reflect the energy efficiency and sustainable positioning of companies.

How Arup is building a better world

'Arup has been in the green business for all of its life,' claims David Singleton. Sixty years ago, the business was established with sustainable principles at its core, although they weren't articulated as such at the time. Indeed, the company was a little reluctant to shout about its credentials, as it was how it had always worked.

Singleton explains how, in late 2007, he managed to convince colleagues on the board to commit to a statement of what Arup stood for with respect to sustainability. 'We agreed and launched … a number of policies that define how we do our business – we have the standard health and safety policy, environment policy and to that we added one on sustainability.'

Over the 60 years, the emphasis has shifted in the ability to design and build what we might now call green buildings. 'At the beginning the focus was more on whole-of-life cost rather than a much bigger agenda of sustainability, and therefore, if we look back, earlier designs might include some less sustainable aspects, because we weren't thinking so broadly.'

The biggest difference is that Arup now seeks to look at building design through the lens of consumers rather than policy, and then find a match between the two. Designers have a passion for both perspectives, which leads to healthy debates and interesting solutions.

Arup has a unique ownership structure. It shares with John Lewis the concept of being owned by staff beneficiary trusts. 'There are no human shareholders in Arup, therefore there are no circumstances where decisions the board might make could be linked to lining their pockets, other than if the firm is financially successful then everybody in the firm will benefit.'

The business, argues Singleton, has always managed for the long term. 'We haven't had individual shareholders within the leadership or, even worse, the stock market looking over our shoulder and wanting to know what our next quarter results are going to be, or a CEO who's got options that will be realized at a particular share price.'

Generation IM's focus on sustainable investing

'Our business was established to exclusively focus on sustainable investing,' explains Colin le Duc. 'Former [US] vice president Al Gore and former Goldman Sachs CEO David Blood founded Generation Investment Management in 2004 to bring together the worlds of finance and sustainability. It is all we do.

'We are a focused boutique investment manager that fully integrates sustainability into a traditional equity research framework. Sustainability is core to everything we do and our investments reflect this commitment. We are managing $4 billion in institutional assets in two funds: Global Equity Fund and the Generation Climate Solutions Fund. We invest in both public and private companies that are part of the solution to sustainability globally.'

Le Duc believes that the best businesses are those that are managed for the long term. 'Within this context it is important to have a vision and a mission that inspire people and customers. By only focusing on financial performance without regard for how that value is created can work in the short term but will ultimately fail long term given fundamental human motivation to create something positive for future generations.

'Strategic decisions that are long term must integrate material sustainability factors. Stakeholder considerations are part of long-term shareholder-value issues and can't be treated as separate in our view. There is no conflict between value and values in the long term.'

Taking the long view with Fairtrade

At the Fairtrade Foundation, Harriet Lamb feels that companies that focus on shareholder value, and particularly a short-term obsession with profits, will over time lose the support of consumers and other stakeholders. 'It is hardly a new idea that companies need constantly to earn their licence to operate, and to invest back in the communities upon whom they depend whether as workers or farmers or customers.

'We can all argue about whether it is the role of companies to tackle poverty and promote sustainable development. We believe it absolutely is; others might disagree. But we are all agreed that it is the role of business to deliver what their customers want; because indeed, the customer is always right. Cafédirect sells only Fairtrade hot beverages and is the UK's fifth-largest coffee company – which is good business by any bottom line.'

When supermarket Sainsbury switched all its bananas to Fairtrade, it created a social premium of around \$7.8 million in 2007, to be returned to the growers and their communities. Sainsbury has also set up a Fair Development Fund so that disadvantaged smallholders can apply to get help in building their businesses or improving their quality. Likewise, Marks & Spencer has engaged with cotton farmers in India and Mali to help them improve quality.

As companies become more aware, and dependent on their relationships with nature, they turn to the WWF for advice. 'I recently met the CEO of the most successful brewery in Columbia. Why are they interested in talking to WWF? Primarily they are concerned about sustainability of access to fresh water, essential to making beer. We have concerns over water beyond beer because the whole ecosystem depends on fresh water. So there is a commonality of interests. Of course they have a commercial interest, but there is still a win-win if we work together.'

A revolution in the world of fashion

'We are at the point of fantastic opportunity, as well as having an acute necessity, to radically rethink the way in which we approach every aspect of our businesses,' says Dilys Williams from London College of Fashion. 'This is a restart situation. A revolution in action, and a call to human ingenuity to find new design, manufacturing and communication paradigms.'

Williams believes fashion has a crucial role to play. 'It holds a powerful place in our existence and it can communicate beauty and feelings that move society forward,' she says. Design is at the centre of this, given that on average 80 per cent of purchase decisions are driven by design. These disciplines, she feels, should be embraced at an early stage in the development of new products, but equally in any other aspect of business – an approach that can be used by all managers, not just specialist designers. In particular, Williams believes that new combinations of business and society, science and art, can produce the most innovative designs.

'There is an interconnection between focusing on the environment and people as benefactors and business growth,' she agrees. 'For fashion design this can be interpreted in a number of ways – from improving efficiency, to reduced overtime, increased wages and conditions leading to increased productivity, lower overall costs and less waste; through to designing attachment into our clothes, thus raising brand identity whilst reducing environmental impact. New technologies such as body scanning, 3-D printing and user-driven design can turn the process on its head and eradicate some of the issues and impacts currently impeding our systems and practices whilst creating a new knowledge economy.'

Business at a cultural crossroads

'Business as a whole desperately needs a purpose beyond financial results,' says Nigel Morris of Aegis, the media communications and market research group. 'Without a mission that is wider than just the financials, businesses are both fragile and brittle. That mission can be a pioneering one in a number of fields.'

He sees society, and indeed culture, at a crossroads. 'The world has got flatter, more connected, more interdependent and in many ways smaller, and yet the structures to help manage and govern this transforming world are just not performing. Politics and politicians all over the world have been devalued through persistent examples of greed, insidious corruption and nepotism. It is all so transparent and people are looking for alternative role models.

'Perhaps the critical factor in the importance of a wider mission is the ability to attract the best talent. With work taking so much of our lives, there will be a blurring of life in and out of work and people will increasingly want to work with organizations that reflect their values and in which they feel they can make a wider difference.'

2 Strategies for growth

- How to evaluate and focus on the most attractive markets.
- How to use sustainability as your competitive advantage.
- How to focus your resources for commercial impact.

Strategy is about making big choices, to align resources and maximize the success of the business in the short and longer term.

Strategy is about focusing on the most profitable markets of the future, ensuring that you secure competitive advantage in them, and can reap the rewards from them. Strategy is about being clear about what you will not do, as importantly as what you will do, defining boundaries and setting priorities. Strategy requires trade-offs to align the competing forces within business and ensure that value is created reasonably for all the diverse stakeholders.

In the changing business world, it is clear that markets that embrace sustainable practices will be the more attractive. There will be two types of sustainable market – adaptive and emergent. In these markets the fiscal incentives will be there, the risks lower, the support greater, and as business is encouraged to exploit sustainable markets, then consumers will follow, shifting demand and the potential for profitable growth. From alternative energy to hybrid cars, healthy foods to ethical banking, business will migrate to good, or at least better, practices and products, reallocating investment and innovation in them, and they in turn will become the coolest, hottest, most desirable items of the future.

From Coca-Cola to GE, Lego to Nike, companies are struggling and striving to make sense of the new world, to set the new agenda, to stand out as the most sustainable in their world. For every company the challenges are different – some more internal than external, some about how, others about why. Energy companies, for example, are the best and worst at it. They rape the Earth and pollute the skies, but they also recognize that their industries will not be here in 50 years unless they fundamentally change products and process, business and beliefs.

Typically it is easier for long-cycle industries to make the change. From aerospace to pharmaceuticals, these types of companies take a strategic approach to investment and innovation, to changing customer mindsets and behaviour over time. Other sectors, like retail and consumer goods, have a much shorter-term outlook, driven by fashion and impulse, and need to ride with 'the wave' towards a sustainable future.

Creating more value for everyone

A sustainable business strategy is one that enables the organization to achieve its purpose and maximize value creation in doing so.

Value is created over time, and therefore requires a sustained approach to investments and profit generation. The value created can be shared between stakeholders – customers and employees, owners and society – in any way. However, in the same way as the business needs to decide how much of its profits to give as bonuses and how much to reinvest in the business, a sustainable business will need to understand how much to share with many more partners, including society itself.

This allocation of money should not be seen as benevolence, rather as a broader (and more enlightened) investment strategy. However, considering the broader impacts on society and its stakeholders requires structure and coordination, so that it delivers a positive return for all, a 'win–win–win' as Nike calls it.

The reality of the 'sustainability' movement more generally is that it is still largely dysfunctional, and therefore unable to work with business in positive ways.

Social and environmental agendas are littered with a multitude of well-intentioned international and local agencies, pressure groups and passionate activists all fighting their corners. They fail to communicate or coordinate with each other, to see the challenge holistically and sometimes the conflicts that they promote. They see things in black and white. Their beliefs can become extreme, and their actions misinterpreted. Their diverse agendas can fragment rather than contribute towards sustainable solutions.

Whilst their intentions are mostly worthy, this leads to confusion for a business seeking to do the right thing. It needs focus to be embedded as part of business strategy. Business needs to create its own infrastructure, working with the bodies most appropriate to its purpose.

At the same time, most companies, products and processes are becoming more sustainable without deliberately thinking about their sustainability. Motivated by lowering costs, improving speed or reducing prices, companies have been getting better because it makes sense financially and competitively.

Supply chains are becoming more efficient, with less waste, because this reduces costs. Food and drinks companies reduce packaging in order to lower transport costs. Automotive manufacturers are designing with lighter frames because consumers want cars that are cheaper to run. Tobacco companies invest huge sums in social initiatives in an effort to offset their unhealthy image. Similarly banks invest in local communities to build goodwill with their customers and employees.

This 'natural' evolution now needs structure and acceleration, realizing the benefits for consumers and business, and exploring what more can be achieved.

Finding markets with sustainable growth

Your challenge is to create a winning business strategy, not a sustainability strategy.

The most effective business strategies will embrace sustainability at their core, fundamentally affecting your decisions about where and how to compete, rather than as a contributory factor or as an afterthought.

The business strategies that secure the most sustainable growth will be those that also embrace the sustainability agenda at its core, sustaining their performance through a more holistic approach to the world in which it operates.

A business strategy has three components:

- Where will you compete (choosing the markets of highest potential value in the mid to longer term on which to focus)?
- What makes you different (identifying the source of your competitive advantage in these chosen markets)?
- How will you make money (developing an appropriate business model that will sustain profitable growth in these markets)?

The point is that these are your choices.

Too many business leaders don't make intelligent choices. They feel limited by convention or bound by history – they compete in markets because their business always has done, or is currently designed to do so, or it would seem foolish not to continue exploiting existing revenue streams, even if they are beginning to dwindle. Choosing is the hardest bit. It's easy to start doing things, much harder to stop doing them.

In a world of complexity and connected forces, strategy is no longer obvious. A distinctive winning business strategy requires careful, broader and more enlightened thought.

The most valuable markets – measured in terms of their growth potential over the next three to five years and your ability to make a profit in them, not necessarily as they are but through your presence and innovation in them – are likely to be those with a sustainable core.

The right markets for you depend on your chosen purpose and the assets already in your business (existing capabilities shouldn't restrict the markets you enter; you can always find a partner with the right capabilities to deliver your vision). You may well find that applying sustainable innovation to existing markets is less attractive than entering new markets that start from the premise of being sustainable, and then commercial, in order to meet the changing needs of customers.

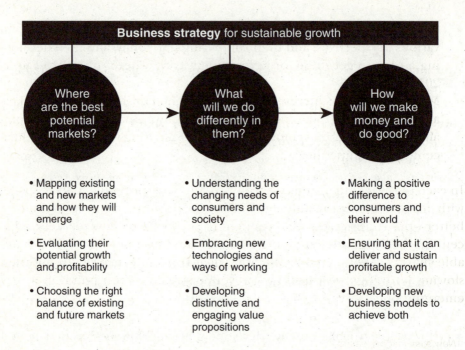

Figure 2.1 Business strategy for sustainable growth: making new choices about where, what and how (source: Genius Works)

The new 'high growth – high profit' markets for your business might include areas such as cleaner energies, efficient technologies, fair-trade goods – and geographies as diverse as India and China, Turkey and Brazil, or many others. But they might equally be established markets, addressed in a different way: innovative products with more sustainable benefits, or a business model that is more inclusive in the way it works with communities and society.

New market spaces

Strategy, and particularly your choice of markets and differentiation within them, is not a regressive, analytic process as many strategists would encourage. It is a creative, divergent and imaginative process. It requires you to 'open up' the scope of possibilities before 'closing down' on the best ones. Unless you extend your initial radar you are likely to miss the best opportunities, particularly when many of tomorrow's most attractive markets lie outside the conventional radar of steady-state businesses.

Two techniques are useful for opening up your strategic thinking:

- Future radar: disruptive thinking, by imagining your world in 2020 from various perspectives, and then comparing it to today, and then developing a plan to get there, or at least identifying where you will get to by 2015;
- Market mapping: incremental thinking, by considering the markets adjacent to yours today, physically (geography, capability) or conceptually (purpose, business model) and then evaluating where the best adjacent opportunities lie.

In each of these dimensions you can 'stretch' your potential market space, with more options to evaluate, but also with more chances of finding better opportunities. As well as opening your eyes to new markets, adjacent markets also offer stepping stones to the brave new world of sustainable markets. They enable you to evolve from one market to another, slowing letting go of a declining revenue stream as you build up a new emerging one.

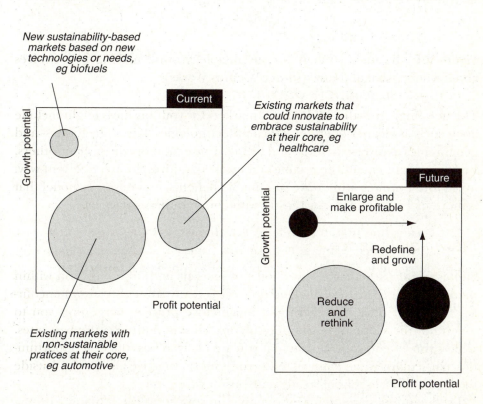

Figure 2.2 Sustainable markets: evaluating sustainable and non-sustainable markets in terms of potential growth and profitability

Creating differentiation by doing good

It's incredibly hard to be different.

Companies spend millions in the pursuit of competitive advantage – on innovation to create the highest-performance products, people to deliver the most personalized services, branded advertising to either communicate these differences or at least create an illusion of them.

The reality is that there is little of lasting difference.

Products and services are often imitated before they are launched, because most innovations are superficial or incremental. Most image-based differentiation is transient as it rides a trend wave that quickly moves on or is quickly uncovered by consumers. As companies struggle to differentiate their products and services, prices inevitably fall, profits erode and business works ever harder to find another gimmick to stay afloat.

Meanwhile product life cycles get ever shorter, more and more is invested in innovation, more and more products are launched, accelerating the consumer's desire for newest and best, and the landfills of perfectly good but unwanted products grow ever higher.

There is a better way – a better way for business, and for the world.

Finding a sustainable advantage

Social and environmental issues are probably the fastest-emerging agenda items for consumers today. Companies seek to achieve competitive advantage in areas that are most important to their consumers. Therefore social and environmental issues offer some of the best opportunities to differentiate.

Differentiation needs to be relevant, important and ideally without compromise.

This means finding the right aspects of the issues that resonate most with the target audience. Climate change, for example, is often too abstract for people to relate to on a day-to-day, product and personal level. Buying local produce that supports local farmers, and without the many 'food miles' of more exotic alternatives, is more meaningful.

The Co-operative Bank is also one of the UK's leading motor insurers. Insurance is a notorious commodity. Every competitor is perceived to offer the same product and service, and therefore everyone shops around for the cheapest price. Co-operative Insurance wanted to be different, and encourage more responsible (cleaner, less) use of the car.

It developed a concept called Eco-Insurance, in which the price would no longer be based on the risk of the driver, as with every other insurance provider, but on the carbon emissions of the car. High-risk consumers (such as the young and those with expensive cars) would for the first time get a low-price insurance if they chose a car with low emissions.

There was coherence across the proposition. For example, the price was lower for those who used their cars less, and who were prepared to use recycled parts for repair. This innovative business model encouraged people to adopt better environmental practices, offered significant differentiation, and gave people a positive reason to choose the brand.

At the same time as supporting a 'good' purpose, people also want the best product, the highest-performance car, the tastiest food or the cheapest clothes. They don't want to compromise.

Green & Black's is a premium chocolate manufacturer. The chocolate is incredibly rich, with high cocoa content. For many years the brand could only be found on the top shelf of health-food stores, promoted as 'organic' and the secret of leading chefs. It was only when the brand was repositioned as 'luxurious and organic' that demand started to grow. Premium retailers clamoured to stock the chocolate, and it became the must-have chocolate.

Toyota's Prius hybrid car was initially perceived as bulky and unattractive, its larger hybrid engine compromising the sleek lines associated with more desirable models. Logically it made sense. Cars are one of the worst day-to-day carbon emitters used by the general public, and the Prius was a simple way of doing better. But emotionally it was a wrench. Until it became cool. Supermodel Naomi Campbell started driving a Prius and others followed. The hybrid became cool. Demand grew, and if there was a compromise, it didn't seem to matter.

New business models for a new business world

Grameen Bank, John Lewis, Novo Nordisk are all examples of more sustainable business models, where the creation of value is done in more collaborative ways with consumers and employees, society and the environment.

However 'business model' is a vastly overused and misunderstood term.

It means the business structure that you choose in order to make money – how the business comes together with its many stakeholders (suppliers, investors, customers, distributors, partners and others) and how costs and revenues (and potentially ideas and other types of impacts, risks and other rewards) flow between them.

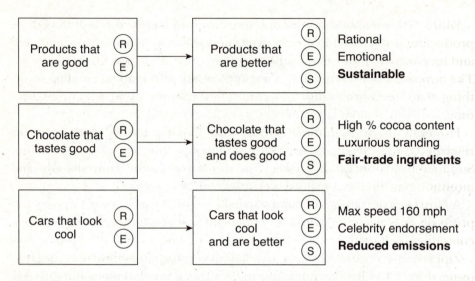

Figure 2.3 Sustainable advantage: embedding social and environmental issues at the heart of products and services

Over the last decade markets have been increasingly disrupted by innovative business models. Skype created a business model that enables free communication over the internet by the consumer and fundamentally challenges the pricing models of traditional communications brands. Ryanair created a business model that enables high-frequency low-priced air travel by outsourcing or eliminating most of its activities, with a devastating impact on existing full-service airlines.

Redesigning business

Applying the concept of business models to the challenges and opportunities of sustainability is an even more disruptive and innovative prospect.

Grameen Bank was founded in Bangladesh in 1983 and has provided 7 million poor people (97 per cent of them women) in 78,000 Bangladeshi villages with $6 billion of small loans to start their own businesses. According to Grameen, 98.6 per cent of these loans have been repaid, and 60 per cent of borrowers have been able to work their way out of poverty. Not only this, but these people now own the business too, the bank's borrowers owning 90 per cent of its shares.

Founder Mohammed Yunus is now replicating his business model around the world. In 2006 his Microcredit Summit Campaign involved 137 countries and seeks to lift half a billion people out of poverty.

Yunus believes in business models that cover their costs through the sale of products and services that meet a market need – there is no loss, no dividend, and investors are motivated by the social benefit rather than financial return. The important point is that it is not about donations but about creating something that is self-sustaining, and continue to deliver its benefits time after time.

However, there is nothing wrong with making money, with investors rewarded with dividends and entrepreneurs achieving personal wealth. Sustainability is not about charity, it is about finding the most effective and motivating mechanics by which a business can do good.

A 'sustainable' business model can take many forms – for-profit, not-for-profit or some form of hybrid. It might put sustainability at its core or as a consequence.

Zipcars, the American car-rental business, challenges the need for car ownership by having cars ready to hire by the minute from locations all over inner cities. After paying a small membership fee, the user pays for time and distance travelled, but doesn't need to pay for ownership or maintenance. It reduces car usage, but more positively for consumers it means they can simply access a cool car whenever they need it, at little cost. The result is fewer cars, reduced emissions and, most significantly for the consumers, cool wheels at an affordable price.

The Arvind Eye Care System of India operates a for-profit business that treats millions of patients every year and has seen rapid profitable growth, but it also allocates some of its profits and the time of its skilled employees to providing resources and training to smaller firms in other countries at no cost. Its profit-making services subsidize services for others who are unable to pay.

Apple and Nokia: being cool in a caring world

Apple and Nokia are both iconic brands that have changed the face of mobile communications, work and entertainment.

Their approaches to environmental and social challenges, however, have followed different paths. Nokia was early to embrace sustainability as a strategic challenge, and one that presented commercial as well as environmental and social opportunities; Apple was stung into action relatively late by criticism from environmental campaigners and its own customers.

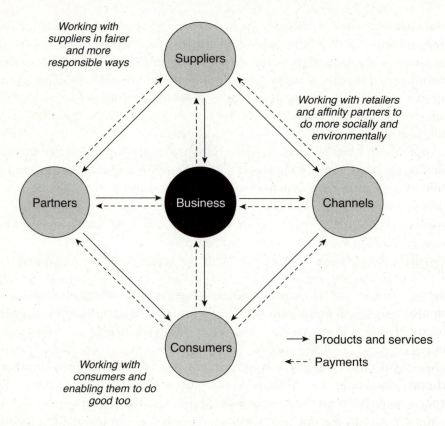

Figure 2.4 Sustainable business models: creating the right business model for you that delivers profitable growth and does good

Both Nokia and Apple have made significant progress in improving the energy efficiency of their products, but both also face a tougher challenge: how to protect profits whilst encouraging users not to throw away their old equipment as soon as a newer, sexier product comes to market.

Apple's challenge

In 2004, Greenpeace launched a campaign to persuade computer manufacturers to reduce electronic waste, to remove the worst toxic substances from their products, to improve their recycling policies and to bring about a fundamental change in the way that electronic products are designed, produced and recycled.

After producing a ranking of manufacturers in 2006, Greenpeace accused Apple of being amongst the slowest to respond, and launched a campaigning website called 'Green My Apple' to enlist the support of Apple's famously loyal customer base. 'Green My Apple' was designed to look like Apple's own site, with in-jokes that only Apple fans would get. 'We love our Macs,' wrote the Greenpeace campaigners. 'We just wish they came in green.' Visitors were encouraged to e-mail Apple CEO Steve Jobs, to link the site to social networking sites, and to come up with their own ideas for greener products. The site won over many Mac users, and prompted Apple to take a hard look at its environmental impacts.

Apple's challenge, as laid down by Greenpeace, was to develop a global take-back scheme, ensure devices were free from toxic chemicals, develop an effective consumer-focused communications strategy to encourage the recyclability of their products, and commit to a track of continuous improvement.

Apple's response

The Greenpeace campaign elicited a swift response from Apple, which subsequently announced its aspiration to become 'an environmental leader'. Apple chose to focus on four areas: product design, responsible manufacturing, energy efficiency and recycling.

Apple's product designers were encouraged to consider environmental criteria – including the need for recyclability – from the start of the design process, and to screen their designs periodically as they progressed.

Apple's manufacturing specialists were briefed to eliminate PVC, arsenic and flame retardants, and to restrict the use of ozone-depleting substances. Apple products were equipped with energy-saving features. Finally, the company introduced a recycling programme that enables consumers to send their old equipment back, free of charge, using either prepaid mail vouchers printable from apple.com, or prepaid envelopes sent by Apple through the mail.

Nokia's challenge

At Nokia, sustainability is viewed and communicated as a business opportunity rather than a barrier or liability.

Nokia's brand mission is to connect people in new and better ways, to help them share life, interests and purpose. Nokia sees this as a challenge for people both within and outside the company, with each person taking small steps that add up to big gains. Nokia calls this concept 'The Power of We'. The extension of responsibility beyond the factory gates to include customers, suppliers and partners is a mark of Nokia's leadership in corporate responsibility. Nokia believes that, in order to be a leader in sustainability, it must help people to make 'sustainable choices'.

A third of all energy used in mobile phones is consumed during the use phase, and up to two-thirds of this can be wasted, so a key challenge for Nokia is to reduce the energy requirements of its phones and chargers, both in terms of their inherent energy efficiency and how they are used by consumers.

Nokia products also contain significant amounts of metals and plastics, the sourcing, manufacture and transport of which use up natural resources (such as oil and water) and release chemicals and greenhouse gases into the natural environment. Nokia's products must also be transported to shops and customers, requiring packaging and further emissions of greenhouse gases.

Nokia's response

Nokia's approach to product design incorporates the use of sustainable and ethically sourced materials, improved energy efficiency, the use of renewable or recycled materials, and the manufacture of recyclable phones. All Nokia phones now remind users to unplug the charger from the mains. Converged products that combine multiple features such as radio, camera, MP3 player and GPS into a single mobile device cut the need for manufacturing, packaging and transport, whilst the ability to download services via the mobile network makes physical software products obsolete. Users can download information on sustainability directly to their phones, and even use their phones to calculate and offset their carbon emissions. Nokia has also developed smaller, lighter packaging and installed a network of almost 5,000 points at which consumers can drop off their old equipment for recycling.

The impact

Thanks to its improved approach to product design, manufacturing, energy efficiency and recycling, Apple products now meet the requirements for the US government's 'Energy Star' rating scheme. Many Apple products now achieve Silver status in EPEAT, a ranking of environmental performance against the 51 criteria laid down in the IEEE1680 international standard scheme. Apple also claims to have prevented the disposal of over 15,000 tonnes of e-waste in landfill sites.

Apple rarely discusses its plans for the future, so it remains to be seen whether the company plans to tackle the challenge of obsolescence, encouraging users to keep their Apple products for longer, rather than replacing them with new models.

Nokia's environmental initiatives and sustainable approach to product design have earned it a place amongst the world's 100 Most Sustainable Corporations according to global100.org, and have accompanied impressive business results; net sales for 2007 of €51,058 million were 24 per cent up on the previous year, and operating profits were up an impressive 45 per cent to €7,985 million. Lighter, smaller packaging has reduced the use of materials by 54 per cent, saving 5,000 truck journeys and saving the company €100 million in shipping costs. Nokia claims that, if all users heed the built-in reminders to switch off phones, enough energy could be saved to power 100,000 average-sized European homes.

Like others in the consumer electronics sector, Nokia has yet to rise to the challenge of 'churn' (the rate at which users replace equipment that is still in good working order).

People, planet, profit: the reality of strategy

Unilever develops a better approach to profitable growth

Santiago Gowland describes some of the challenges of taking these issues into the mainstream business thinking of Unilever.

'Deepening the understanding of social, economic and environmental considerations has become critical as an insight to fuel innovation at every aspect of our businesses' value chains.

'Understanding the ripple effects of business decisions at each operating company or product or brand level is key to develop interventions that can minimize negatives and maximize positive impacts.'

In Unilever his team has been focused on articulating and quantifying these business impacts, first through a collaborative study with Oxfam in Indonesia, focusing on poverty-alleviation linkages and later through a recent study conducted by INSEAD in Unilever's operating company in South Africa, using input–output tables. Both studies have helped the business to better understand the impact of its operations.

Unilever has also developed a 'gaining insights' tool to work at product and brand levels and integrate social, economic and environmental considerations into brand innovation. 'We called this process Brand Imprint, which recognizes that brands satisfy not only [consumers'] functional and emotional needs but their desires and aspirations as citizens as well, and [we] believe that such brands will win over those that don't.'

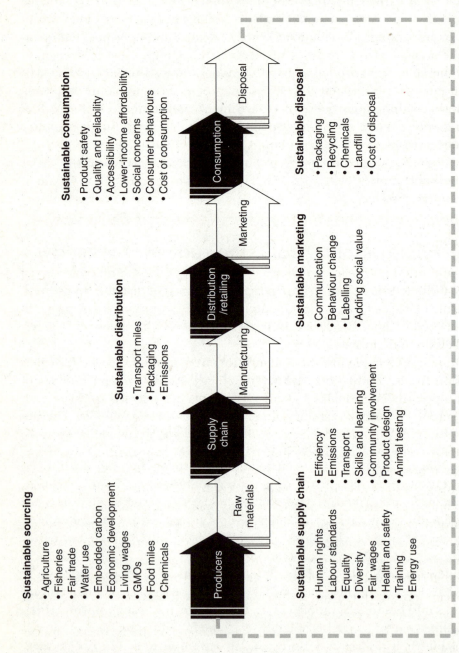

Sustainable sourcing
- Agriculture
- Fisheries
- Fair trade
- Water use
- Embedded carbon
- Economic development
- Living wages
- GMOs
- Food miles
- Chemicals

Sustainable consumption
- Product safety
- Quality and reliability
- Accessibility
- Lower-income affordability
- Social concerns
- Consumer behaviours
- Cost of consumption

Sustainable distribution
- Transport miles
- Packaging
- Emissions

Sustainable disposal
- Packaging
- Recycling
- Chemicals
- Landfill
- Cost of disposal

Sustainable marketing
- Communication
- Behaviour change
- Labelling
- Adding social value

Sustainable supply chain
- Human rights
- Labour standards
- Equality
- Diversity
- Fair wages
- Health and safety
- Training
- Energy use
- Efficiency
- Emissions
- Transport
- Skills and learning
- Community involvement
- Product design
- Animal testing

Producers · Raw materials · Supply chain · Manufacturing · Distribution /retailing · Marketing · Consumption · Disposal

Figure 2.5   Unilever's holistic approach: illustrates an integrated programme of sustainability in every aspect of business (source: Unilever)

Gowland takes a holistic perspective, arguing that 'Everything that exists can be traced back to the nature or essence of human beings; business is a human activity, therefore you can look at business through human lenses and discover that by integrating all of human powers you can obtain a much stronger result.'

At the same time, profitable growth remains the essential aim of Unilever. 'Without good performance, the whole idea of business would be destroyed. However, aligning financial results to positive societal outcomes (what we call 'doing well by doing good') has tremendous power because you enter into a virtuous cycle in which, rather than extracting value from communities and the environment, you are creating value for them, for your employees, your partners and shareholders.'

Generation IM finds that sustainable markets deliver better returns

Generation IM invests in companies that are part of the solution to sustainability. Colin le Duc explains: 'One reason for this is that demand for green is, by virtue of the fact that environmental issues are not unfortunately going to be solved any time soon, robust on a secular level. This means that green markets are here to stay.

'Our clients include institutional investors from around the world, such as pension funds, foundations and family offices. We also have a number of high-net-worth individuals as clients. They have all selected to invest with Generation because of our commitment and focus on sustainability. They do not see a trade-off in financial returns because we are sustainability investors, quite the contrary as we are committed to delivering outstanding investment results above the market.'

Solving the climate crisis, he believes, requires the entire economy to shift from a high-carbon to a low-carbon modus operandi. 'Demand and markets for products and services that enable this shift to occur will be very strong for long periods. Companies that are active in renewable energy, carbon markets, biomass conversion or demand-side efficiency are particularly well positioned to benefit from long-term secular demand for their products and services.

'Green has driven enormous innovation in the financial services industry. The emergence of carbon trading is the most visible example. Across the spectrum of financial services issues of sustainability have driven product development. For example, there are many clean-tech venture funds globally, various insurance products related to climate change, mutual funds with an emphasis on sustainability, amongst many other innovations. Huge numbers are involved too; Citigroup and Bank of America have committed $50 billion and $25 billion respectively over the next 10 years to addressing the climate crisis.'

Kraft's strategy with commitment and a vested interest

'At Kraft we want sustainability to be part of every major business decision that we make,' says the company's Jonathan Horrell. 'The way we put it is "It's good for people, the environment and our business."

'This is a strategy that we've been developing over the years. It says that if you do sustainability right, it's an opportunity to manage your business better, to improve your supply chains, to reinforce quality, to delight your consumers and customers, meet their expectations, as well as to do the right thing.

'We take this strategy and assess where our major impacts are. It won't surprise you to know that for a food business these are energy (and therefore carbon emissions), water use, waste and packaging, distribution and of course the agricultural commodities that we buy for all our products.

'First of all, we look to see what we can do to reduce these impacts. We use a combination of reporting and target setting to guide this. Second, this helps us to design better processes, for example for using less water, less energy, and less packaging. For example, all our packaging designers use a tool that calculates the environmental impact.

'We have an ethical commitment and a vested interest. Our company values dictate that we do the right thing – shareholders expect us to deliver value, so we can't make sacrifices on behalf of an ideal. We have ethically pragmatic but also deep-rooted values. It is a mix, but must also fit the business.'

Green to gold with a carrot and a stick

Dan Esty, author of *Green to Gold*, believes that 'Green issues have become a critical element of corporate strategy for most companies and most industries. There are a number of drivers that have changed business attitudes towards the environment. First, high energy prices have made efficiency and energy conservation a critical priority for almost every business – and for that matter for almost every household. Second, the prospect of new regulations driving up other costs has focused many companies on the need to be more careful, particularly with their energy consumption. The reality of carbon charges in some form adds to the high energy prices a further logic for efficiency. Companies are also recognizing that they need to be attentive to their resource productivity for all of the inputs to their products.

'But we have also found that the strongest logic for a vigorous environmental element to a business plan comes from the opportunity to increase shareholder value,' he says. Indeed, the talk about a 'triple bottom line' seems to be fading. The strongest logic for a 'green to gold' strategy is the business logic.

Esty describes how some companies are finding that nature is impinging on their business opportunities. 'If you are Coca-Cola, and are dependent on water for your business, then the prospect of climate change that might shift rainfall patterns can be quite threatening. A company like this needs a climate-change policy whether governments are stepping up to the issue or not.'

He also points to the many diverse stakeholders that care about environmental issues. 'This goes way beyond the traditional focus of governments and environmental groups.' He believes that employees see corporate attitudes to the environment as symbolic of how companies treat their own people too, and likewise with customers. But his experience is that business can influence huge change. 'When a CEO like Lee Scott of Wal-Mart insists on reduced packaging, less waste, improved energy efficiency and lower greenhouse gas emissions, every one of the 60,000 suppliers to Wal-Mart has to raise their game.'

An alternative to unsustainable consumerism

'The industrial model that morphed into the mass "consumerization" of society is fundamentally unsustainable,' believes Aegis's Nigel Morris, who helps his clients rethink their brands and communications in a better way. 'We have ended up creating, producing and consuming too much that we don't need and even don't want. This may seem counter-intuitive but we have created a disposable culture with disposable products, and profits often driven by built-in obsolescence. We all know that this cannot go on for environmental reasons, but from a well-being perspective, the more we are consuming and the faster we are consuming, the unhappier and less satisfied we are becoming.

'The new model will be to create products that have more intrinsic value, that last longer and provide more benefit to consumers. In that way "green" markets will be seen as more valuable by consumers and will generate advantage and greater profitability.'

However, Morris is sure that unsustainable 'consumerization' does not mean an end to growth. 'Macroeconomic growth is absolutely vital to the future of the planet and its people. What has to change are the drivers of growth and the outputs of that growth. There is so much economic activity that needs to happen that can have a positive effect. Governments lack the moral courage to see past the next opinion poll, so much of the pressure will come from consumers and forward-thinking visionary businesses.'

Choosing the best markets at Arup

Arup sees its strategic focus on sustainable building design as making most business sense. Across the world, from Canada to China, it is the premium sector in its markets and is seen as a leader in the field. Its advantage is that it has all the capabilities under one roof – research and development, design and management – and globally too.

'We make significant investments in researching the future of work and changing lifestyles,' says David Singleton. 'They are built into our cost structures. We are not the cheapest firm by any means. What we would argue, and I think we can point to it with virtually 100 per cent justification, is that people want to use Arup because of the things we can bring to the party, which they can justify to their purchasing committee, paying a little more for it.'

Geographically, Arup is finding huge interest in sustainability in mainland China, but many others are not yet committed to sustainable principles. 'In their three-to-five-year plan they talked about sustainability – they might have used another term for it – but they talked about it virtually all the way through. It's very clearly a part of their thinking. The government is committed. They've got to build all these new places for people to live, and they want to do so in as sustainable a fashion as they can.'

One of Arup's highest-profile developments is the eco-city of Dontang, off the coast from Shanghai. 'Dontang represents a model solution for them. It's so ambitious; there must be some questions about whether it can actually happen. But conceptually it's sound, and it has a huge amount of support.' Meanwhile there are many similar developments in smaller cities, embracing 90 per cent of the concepts, demonstrating consistency of approach.

Nike's system thinking for more impact

Nike moved from seeing sustainability as a supply-chain challenge to business opportunity when it embraced 'system thinking' – moving away from thinking about business functions, and separate issues like labour, community and environment.

Hannah Jones, VP of Sustainability at Nike, found it a revelation. Her sustainability team became part of the business strategy, planning and innovation teams.

'My concern is that we are seeing a lot of companies doing incredible things – but it's one thing or the other, but not necessarily marrying the systems thinking into the business strategy.' Jones particularly admires the approaches of Wal-Mart and M&S. 'Wal-Mart has the power to effect scale change and for Lee Scott to take someone who was in charge of their sustainability team and put them in charge of their Home brand is awesome.' Meanwhile at M&S, she admires the holistic approach of their Plan A and its communication to consumers.

'When you look at a business model and you think about it as a system or a kind of ecosystem in and of itself, you realize that it's all interconnected and I can find environmental solutions for working rights and vice versa, and also that as long as you are sitting in a system, if you are at the end of the process, you're always trying to retrofit something that has already happened. If I can influence that front end, then I can influence the entire business model. It's a much easier lever to pull.'

3 Inspiring leadership

- How to lead your business in an age of crisis and change.
- How to ensure you become an effective role model.
- How to influence and inspire people to follow.

Too many leaders have their heads down, making them good project managers, controlling the status quo, ensuring that plans are delivered and targets achieved. They are good at focusing on the short term, working within the existing rules.

Too many leaders put their commercial blinkers on when they go to work.

At home they are real people, who care about the world around them, their families and communities, fairness and ethics. But when they step into their office, their conscience is put to one side. They are focused on their isolated little world – their sector, product, department, project, timescales. They lose sight of the bigger picture.

Today's leaders must do business with their heads up, sensing and interpreting the evolving world around them, sensitive to the needs and priorities of others inside and outside their business, to make new connections and brilliant compromises, and have the ability to see the new opportunities as they emerge.

Today's leaders must embrace a new mindset for business, one that thinks sustainably about their success, more innovatively and holistically, and more proactively and responsibly.

Imaginative leaders

In the same way that Leonardo da Vinci designed technologies for future generations, so Jeff Immelt's 'Ecomagination' encouraged an old conventional business to reawaken the entrepreneurial spirit of Thomas Edison, and define new solutions for the coming age.

Table 3.1   New leadership mindset: from old attitudes about sustainability to a realization about the difference sustainability can make

Old sustainability mindset	New sustainability mindset
Non-core	Core
Threat	Opportunity
Compliance	Innovation
Cost	Profit
Incremental	Breakthrough
Local and caring	Global and responsible
Multiple responses	Systemic solutions
Reactive	Proactive
Conflicting	Complementary
Unquantifiable	Quantifiable
Long term	Short and long term

In 2005 GE started to think more strategically about climate change and how it could affect its business and that of its customers. Immelt was an active champion, recognizing it as a market force that was reshaping the competitive landscape, not just a good thing to do. GE launched 'Ecomagination', which became a coordinated programme of innovation, a new portfolio of products and services, that embraced clean technologies in every sector. GE sought to double annual investments in clean technologies to $1.5 billion by 2010, with at least $20 billion incremental revenues. It is well on its way to achieving this, most significantly with an increase in profitability.

Yet it is rarely those with power and prestige who see the light. Challenged by the provocation of the likes of Sir Bob Geldoff and Al Gore, the established world is now beginning to see things differently. In the same way as Alexander Fleming saw bacteria on his Petri dish and rethought it as penicillin, so Richard Branson sees algae and reinterprets it as rocket fuel.

'Heads up' leaders are forward thinkers, open minded, more collaborative, less hierarchical.

They appreciate the value of being different, the value of conflicting ideas and opinions, the value of situations that at first may seem negative but can be reinterpreted in more positive ways. They can cope with uncertainty and ambiguity. They can address problems more systematically, and develop more holistic or connected solutions. They can turn a threat into an opportunity. And they themselves are role models with more enlightened attitudes and efficient personal behaviours.

Great leaders inspire followers. The new business world needs new business leaders.

The same traits that give the new leader personal inspiration to make sense of their world and to make better choices are also what other people find inspiring. People are inspired by leaders who can articulate a positive vision, who can rise above the squabbling of short-term issues to give a clear and compelling direction. Their vision inspires people because it is inclusive, it sells the benefits to them, it explains why it is better than what we have today, and gives them the courage to start taking steps towards a better world.

Leaders of the new business world

Leadership and management are different things.

Managers get things done

Management is much more about 'getting things done'. It is therefore a much more mechanical, linear and quantitative approach, driven by processes and controls, with clearly defined tasks and measurable outputs. It thrives on planning, organizing, delivering and controlling.

Managers break down a strategic vision into finite tasks, focusing on the detail and practicality of making things happen, step by step, day by day. It is a tactical mindset. It is about effective decision making, effective delivery – on time, to cost, driving quarterly revenues.

Managers are much more likely to say no than yes. If sustainability is left to management, to be embraced as part of rational operational processes, then it is likely to remain a threat rather than an opportunity, about compliance rather than innovation.

However, a manager's success is by definition only achieved through others. Motivation is therefore a crucial attribute, understanding what makes people tick, understanding how to behave in a way that engages people – those whom they manage directly but also peers across the organization and their own managers.

'Middle management' often becomes an organization bottleneck – as it is these people who translate visions into reality, turn strategic priorities into daily tasks, communicate key messages up and down the organization, balance and connect the many different activities, and allocate scarce resources for most impact. Middle managers are the organization enablers, the politicians and the engine room. In making change happen, in improving effectiveness, in making dreams come true, they are often the most important but frequently overlooked people in the business.

Leaders inspire others

Leadership is the other side of management.

Management and leadership are the 'yin and yang' of large organizations. Whilst management is more heads down, focus and control, leadership is heads up, vision and connections. Leaders provide the inspiring vision that makes people want to follow them. They pull rather than push, they engage and energize people in a higher purpose, an inspiring vision, in seeing what is possible.

Leadership can be loud or quiet, rallying people from the podium or influencing them personally.

Whilst management likes structure and process, hierarchies and boxes, leadership is more fluid, it brings people together, often from different parts and levels of the organization. It connects ideas and people, who together can do much more than they could apart. A leader might be hands on, playing a specialist role, particularly in the early stages, or hands off, more of a facilitator and coach.

A sustainable business therefore needs inspired leadership, with the energy and perspective to encourage people to rethink, to reach out to the world around them, to reject the limitations of established practices and create a better world.

The successful business leaders of the 21st century, in big companies and small, share some common characteristics – combining the passion and directness of the entrepreneur with the rigour and discipline of the corporate executive.

They personify the five Cs of the new business leader:

- *Communicator* *of vision:* articulating a clear and inspiring direction for the business, living the values and personality of the .brand, engaging all stakeholders in active dialogues. Externally they will be ambassadors of the brand – engaging stakeholders and partners – and the human face of the business to the media.
- *Connector* *of people:* bringing the best people and best ideas together – internally as well as from other companies and specialists – to generate bigger and better ideas and solutions. They will focus on building great teams, putting the right people in the right jobs for today and planning for future succession.
- *Catalyst* *of change:* constantly seeking new possibilities, challenging the business to think differently, to be more innovative and effective, faster and with more impact. This might be in the form of provocative ideas and disruptive challenges, and being prepared to play devil's advocate rather than being a rule maker.
- *Coach* *of high performance:* working with and supporting all levels across the organization, in their boardrooms and shop floors, and even with peers in other companies. The leader adds their own specialist skills to the business – their brains, technical knowledge, previous experiences, insights and instincts.
- *Conscience* *of business:* deciding what is right and wrong, considering the big picture of the company and its role, and how it can help create a better world, championing business ethics and corporate responsibility, cultural diversity, equal opportunities, staying true to the business purpose and brand values.

The new business leader will be a leader and manager, executive and entrepreneur:

Heads-down leaders	Heads-up leaders
Leading by control	Leading by inspiration
Managing the steady state	Managing sustained growth
Ensuring consistency	Catalyst of change
Reserved and controlling	Passionate and energizing
Cautious and corporate	Open and personal
Doing work	Overseeing work
Managing hierarchically	Facilitating communities
Process and tasks	Knowledge and innovation
Doing what always done	Embracing ideas from outside
Enforcing regulations	Reinventing the rules
Products and transactions	People and relationships
Evaluating past performance	Supporting future performance
Generating more sales	Creating extraordinary value

The new business leader recognizes that business growth also requires personal growth, and that a sustainable business leader must also be a role model, leading a sustainable lifestyle.

Leaders as the catalysts of change

Taking the big leaps to become a sustainable business is possible only with inspired leadership. And whilst change might well happen through many small steps, it has to first overcome the status quo, the conventions of business as usual, and the natural preferences of managers to work within the world that they know.

When Barack Obama spent two years travelling the big cities and small towns of the United States, looking for votes to become the next president, it was easy to make promises.

In a country that had lost much of its conscience and confidence thanks to the oil-based protective capitalism of Texan George Bush, Obama offered a new vision to the millions of people who lived in poverty and aspired to equal opportunities. He offered a new direction to those who cared about their environment, but were hampered by a president in denial about even the basic facts of climate change.

Obama took office on a wave of hope. But he also had to start delivering on promises amidst the worst economic conditions of a century. It would have been easy to delay the good promises until he had sorted out the financials, but he didn't. He recognized, and made others see, that the two were connected. He committed record-breaking government investments in healthcare and education, clean technologies and emission reductions.

Through new incentives he encouraged business to see these as opportunities for innovation and growth at a time when older industries were on their deathbeds.

Yes, we can

Back at GE, Jeff Immelt used his popularity in his early days to establish his vision as reality, and his core review of his business to start making it happen. He knew he would live or die by it, but he also knew that it was what the business needed, and he personally needed to be the one to make it happen.

He rolled his sleeves up and sat for hours in innovation workshops with his managers, in meetings with key clients exploring their issues and ideas. He challenged conventions and assumptions, and encouraged people to think more broadly and differently.

Change, for most people, is scary and uncertain. The existing world feels much safer and certain. In reality, the opposite is true. There is no ideal time for change, although a crisis can give you a reason which is not often tangible in good times. Whilst people might intellectually want to change, few middle managers stick their necks out.

Sustainable leaders must be bold and brave – taking the big leaps, and taking others with them.

What it means personally

Everybody knows what car the boss drives, the frequency with which they fly around the world, where they work and what they do, the clothes they wear and the food they eat. When you are a leader of a large business with many important challenges, these things might seem trivial or idealistic, but they are the symbols of what really matters.

Leadership is about followership.

If you want your managers to really think about environmental challenges as the stimulus for innovation, or how the business can become a leader in clean technologies, then driving up to work in a high-emission 4×4 SUV sends out completely the wrong message.

If you want your managers to adopt more sustainable practices internally, to spend more time in local communities or to recycle paper, then sitting in a remote office with closed door, air conditioning and reams of paper is not the way to go.

Leadership can be symbolic, but it also needs to be genuine.

If you are really committed to a world where business is the driving force of positive change, improving fairness and equality, relieving poverty locally and globally, and reducing carbon emissions by 80 per cent by 2050, then it means committing to better personal behaviours too.

It starts with you

Of course, there are many guides that offer you '50 ways to green your life', to forget the Caribbean beach, to use low-energy light bulbs and turn vegetarian, but here are some simple yet effective challenges for you as a business leader:

1. Drive smarter. Everyone knows what car the boss drives, so consider trying a hybrid or even electric, or you could get on your bike. That would say something.
2. Travel less. Executives spend half their lives travelling, so take up the WWF 20 per cent less challenge, offset your emissions, or use video conferencing more often.
3. Work together. Self-important offices isolate you from reality, need more heating in cold times and more air conditioning in warm months. Get out and meet your people.
4. Recycle it. So much for the paperless office. We still love the stuff, but try printing half size or double sided, choose chlorine-free paper, and recycle it.
5. Learn to live it. What you do outside work is less visible to the world, but still matters. 'Recycle, reduce and reuse' because you really care, not just for show.
6. New vacations. That would be a talking point – rejecting the exotic long-haul beach in favour of climbing nearby mountains, rediscovering your locality.
7. Live well. It makes you feel better and shows you care. Get down to the gym, run to work occasionally, choose fresh fruit not biscuits, reduce your caffeine, drink green tea.
8. Go local. Encourage local food in the staff restaurant – more healthy but more interesting too. Reduce your food miles and support local farmers and traders.
9. Give some time. Just occasionally do something good for others – a few hours on a community project, raising money for charity, doing your bit.

10. Smile. Easiest of all, and with most impact, smile a little more – it transforms how people feel, changes their attitude to work, and you will feel better too.

Small things might seem inconsequential. But they make a difference. They shape your attitudes, and that changes your outlook. The world can't wait for governments to make our lives better, and business can't wait for people to evolve naturally. It starts with you.

Patagonia and Timberland: reaching new heights

US companies Patagonia and Timberland are both closely connected with the environment, because of the nature of their products, the types of people who buy those products, and the commitment of their staff to environmental and social challenges. In a world where many brands are jumping on the green bandwagon, Patagonia and Timberland have both had to find effective ways of differentiating themselves and demonstrating their longer-standing commitment. Both have also used consumers to fuel positive organizational change.

Patagonia's challenge

Patagonia, a privately owned US-based company manufacturing and selling outdoor clothing, was an early pioneer of 'corporate environmentalism'. Since 1985, Patagonia has donated $25 million to over 1,000 organizations, and it currently donates at least 1 per cent of its profits to an alliance called 1 per cent For the Planet, which it co-founded. Patagonia often features environmental campaigns in its catalogues and advertising campaigns, such as against oil drilling in sensitive parts of Alaska, 'Ocean as a Wilderness' and 'Don't dam Patagonia'. In early 2008, Patagonia was named 'Eco Brand of the Year' at the Volvo Ecodesign Forum awards in Munich.

According to Patagonia, it aims to make a 'net positive' impact on the environment. Environmental values are more important to Patagonia than to most other brands, for three reasons: Patagonia's founder, Yvon Chouinard, was a keen outdoorsman even before he founded the company in 1972; Patagonia's products are designed for use in nature; and Patagonia's customers are buying those products to help them enjoy nature.

Because Patagonia's customers are more than averagely attached to the environment, it is essential that they trust the company's commitment to environmental stewardship. If that trust were betrayed, the consequences for Patagonia's sales and reputation would be severe. For all of these reasons, Patagonia has incorporated environmental objectives into its corporate mission statement: 'Build the best product, cause no unnecessary harm, and use business to inspire and implement solutions to the environmental crisis.'

Patagonia's response

Patagonia is in the enviable position of having implemented environmental policies and practices long before they became a popular subject for advertisers; it implemented a thorough audit of its environmental impacts throughout the supply chain. Understanding the value that this held for its customers and stakeholders, Patagonia then used this information as a basis for a more transparent and accountable approach to production and marketing, confident that it was not indulging in greenwash.

For example, in 1996 Patagonia risked 20 per cent of its sales by switching from intensively farmed cotton to the less environmentally damaging organic variety, following an environmental study of its supply chain. Because organic cotton was significantly more expensive to produce, Patagonia was faced with either passing these costs on to its customers or cutting its own margins and thereby risking its competitiveness in a crowded market. In fact it did both: price rises were capped at 2 per cent and the company's directors accepted lower margins to cover the rest of the additional cost. To justify the price rises, and to stimulate supply (which was severely restricted at the time), Patagonia communicated the benefits of organic cotton to its customers and worked with partners and suppliers for an expansion in organic cotton production.

More recently, Patagonia created an online application called The Footprint Chronicles, which allows users to explore the supply-chain intricacies of selected products, beginning with how they are sourced and continuing through each step of their international production and manufacture. Consumers can get information about how far their garments have travelled before they reach their local retailer, and assess the progress that has been made or promised in improving the most significant environmental impacts.

Patagonia also created a blog called The Cleanest Line, intended for 'dialogue about the products we build, the sports we love and the environmental issues we're concerned about'. Run ('transparently') by the company itself, The Cleanest Line is intended to be a 'micro-community in which employees, customers and other stakeholders can have open and frank discussions, build relationships, and find common ground in their shared values'.

Timberland's challenge

The Timberland Company evolved in the United States from one founded by the Swartz family in 1918 to manufacture boots. Following the huge success of its Timberland boot in the 1960s, the company extended its appeal beyond its traditional utilitarian values to succeed in fashion footwear, then extended its product range to include clothes and accessories, and began a successful expansion into new territories (especially in Europe).

As an organization that had always placed environmental stewardship at the heart of its business model, Timberland's challenge has been to differentiate itself in a market where environmental claims and messages have come into vogue.

Timberland's response

The opportunity for Timberland lay in communicating its heritage as a long-standing respecter of the environment. Focusing on this heritage – which began with a utilitarian product, turned it into a fashion item, then engaged with environmental values more broadly and deeply – Timberland now summarizes its values in three words: 'Boot, Brand, Belief'. Jeffrey Swartz, the third CEO of Timberland and descendent of the first two, has intensified Timberland's focus on building and sustaining strong communities in three areas: engaged citizenship, global human rights and environmental stewardship. All three are brought together in Timberland's groundbreaking 'nutrition label'. This sticker, carried on every shoe box, tells consumers how much energy was used in producing the shoes, as well as how much of that energy was derived from renewable resources. It also carries information about social performance, with a record of factory audits, ethical labour, and community hours served by Timberland employees (119,776 in 2006).

The impact

Many organizations fear the repercussive effects of addressing their larger impacts, choosing instead to highlight more trivial or incidental ones. By confronting its impacts directly and adopting a more transparent and consultative approach, Patagonia has been able to avoid significant accusations of greenwash. Instead, its customers are generally loyal and happy to recommend the brand to their peers.

Patagonia's strategy appears to favour evolution over revolution. As it seeks to improve the environmental impacts of its operations and supply chain, Patagonia has been smart enough to sign its customers up to the journey, promoting understanding and providing commercial impetus for further change.

Timberland's environmental programme – and its nutritional label in particular – has brought several important benefits: it has allowed the company to set ambitious targets for the reduction of energy use and other environmental impacts (including a commitment to cut carbon emissions by 50 per cent between 2006 and 2010); it raises consumer awareness of the issues; it enables consumers to make informed purchasing decisions; it sets Timberland apart from its competitors in ways that are valued by its consumers; it makes consumers feel part of the solution; and it improves staff recruitment, retention and morale. (In 2007, CNN named Timberland one of the hundred best companies to work for, and the best employer in the state of New Hampshire.)

Importantly, Timberland has also raised the bar for others in the footwear, apparel and fashion industries.

People, planet, profit: the reality of leadership

Nike, designed by the CEO

At Nike the CEO is very much a leader and driver of sustainable thinking. However, according to Hannah Jones, 'Mark Parker is also an amazing thought partner, a challenger,' whilst also getting huge support from founder and chairman Phil Knight and the board. Indeed, board meetings focus on sustainability for at least two hours each month, alongside considering it within every other issue.

Back in 1998, at the height of Nike's 'sweatshop' labour crisis, Knight, at that time the CEO, went out and said it was clear to him that successful companies in the 21st century needed to embrace corporate responsibility and build it into their business strategy. 'We've taken it to heart, and that's why I think we can thrive in the sustainable economy.'

The approach to sustainable leadership is carefully delegated. 'We mapped out the business model and the departments we knew we had to influence and work with, with one member of the sustainability team working with each of these key areas. Design sits in the design function and is co-managed by myself and the design lead. Labour rights are co-managed between myself and one of the top people on sourcing, which means that we sit together every month and we create a triangulated strategy – focused on environment, social and economic issues.'

Dialogue is the only way to overcome the initial business response of 'Yes, I know it matters, but it's going to kill my margin.' Measuring sustainability matters because new numbers give you something new to talk about, something to balance the power of dollar signs. Nike keeps coming back to sustainability as an engine of growth, and then innovation as the way to overcome any conflicts and trade-offs along the way.

Personal passion and commitment

'I believe it is impossible for a company to move toward a serious environmental strategy without having leadership from the very top,' says Dan Esty. 'In the hundreds of companies that we looked at all around the world, we found no examples where a company succeeded with a Green to Gold initiative where the CEO and other top executives weren't personally and deeply committed.'

Esty has found that the companies that take the environment seriously and try to manage these issues systematically do best. 'Companies that think they can address environmental issues by appointing someone as the environmental director and putting them off in a corner generally do not succeed.'

The most successful approaches, he says, integrate environmental thinking into all elements of the business. 'Of course, this requires leadership from the top and a commitment to help managers at all levels figure out how to make environment part of their everyday operations.'

Arup reorganizes itself to drive sustainability

Arup is managed by a group board of 12 directors, each committed to sustainable building development. 'Some of us, in addition to having day jobs, like chairman of infrastructure – which is my day job – have additional roles,' says David Singleton. 'One of mine is as group sustainability director. So I guess ownership of the policy and the strategy for Arup Group as a whole currently rests with me. The new role has given me a new lease of life.'

Singleton works with each region to develop a strategy to implement the policy in all its projects in ways that are culturally and commercially appropriate for each market. These are championed by regional sustainability directors, acting as the bridge between the global strategy and local operations. 'We put together strategic frameworks for each region, and use the policy framework as the basis for their strategy, which can differ.'

Making better decisions at Generation IM

Everyone at Generation Investment Management is inevitably focused on sustainability, because of its single-minded approach to sustainable investing. 'Our chairman Al Gore leads our efforts and this permeates throughout the organization. Our advisory board also provides important insights into long-term global sustainability trends, which helps our investment team make wiser decisions based on a deeper understanding of the emerging context for business.

'Collaborating with other investors and stakeholders is important in raising the profile of sustainability investing. We have collaborated with various investor initiatives to highlight the relevance of sustainability to the capital markets. These include ASrIA (Association for Sustainable and Responsible Investment in Asia), the Carbon Disclosure Project, the Enhanced Analytics Initiative and the Principles of Responsible Investment amongst others.'

WWF's approach to dealing with complex trade-offs

David Nussbaum knows better than most how difficult and complex sustainability issues can be. There are no simple answers, which means that leaders need to approach these challenges in a different way to other business problems. They need to explore more options, engage with more partners, and sometimes have the guts to do what nobody else has done. They also need to take great care, given the fragility of corporate and brand reputations.

He highlights the complicated trade-offs that leaders will frequently face.

'We are familiar with the theme that flying food from abroad doesn't look terribly good for the environment, and in principle that's right. On the other hand, if you are going to get it domestically and it's going to use a lot more energy domestically than flying internationally, that's a bit more difficult. So how do we deal with that if we've got something that is energy-intensive to create but low-energy to use? Are these assumptions right?'

Similarly, the rapid advance in renewable energies and clean technologies makes it increasingly difficult to know which approaches to back, where to focus investment. He highlights such dilemmas in order to demonstrate the much more difficult decision-making tasks faced by business leaders. They need to make the right choices, have the knowledge to do so, and the ability to explain them to others too.

The most successful businesses in sustainability, according to Nussbaum, are those where the people right at the top are clearly committed to driving this agenda. 'If you think of HSBC where we have a partnership, Stephen Green, the executive chairman, is clearly and absolutely on board on this agenda. If you think about Marks & Spencer, Stuart Rose absolutely identifies with Plan A. No one thinks this is just a sideline interest of the CSR people.'

However, he also believes that these issues can be championed by people in any place in the organization. 'There's no reason for people to feel that just because you are not in charge of everything you can't really make a difference and make an impact. And that can often be by starting small and quickly trying to grow it. Starting with basic recycling, looking at waste, looking at food use, looking at energy consumption and so on. And saying, "OK, we've achieved that, what else can we do?"'

Everyone is a sustainable leader in Unilever

'Everybody in Unilever champions these issues to some extent,' says Santiago Gowland, arguing that otherwise they would never become integrated into the fabric of business as usual. However, he also argues that the CEO makes it all essential, and provides an umbrella under which economic, social and environmental initiatives come together.

'We can do this because our business has massive social impacts. We are in the business of providing nutrition, hygiene and personal care. These are very elemental everyday needs, everywhere. Preventing disease, enhancing health and nutrition, fostering self-belief are business-direct impacts for us. This is what we do. So, everybody working for a brand, in R&D, marketing or in supporting functions has ownership of this agenda.'

In terms of broader issues, such as packaging and climate change, Unilever encourages its businesses to talk with competitors – to level the playing field at a more sustainable basis.

'We need to look into this with real integrity. Trying to turn everything into a competitive advantage can be very detrimental to society. A careful assessment of what needs to be tackled through cross-industry cooperation is critical to the speed of transformation that is needed.'

Part 2

Reconnecting business

'It is not the strongest or most intelligent species that survive, but the ones who are most willing to adapt,' said Charles Darwin.

My world: Sugito, the Japanese salesman

Sugito is 32 years old and lives in Tokyo, Japan with his girlfriend. He works in sales and PR and has a strong interest in design.

When asked about top-of-mind green behaviour, Sugito says, 'Less rubbish, less air conditioning, no McDonald's'. It is within Japanese culture to eat seasonal local food and there are very strict regulations with regards to recycling, so these are easy to do, though not prompted by any motivation to be green.

Sugito would like to buy a hybrid car but it's too expensive. He travels mainly by bicycle. He also loves the idea of being a 'green guerrilla!' and says, 'I sometimes spread seeds of plants where I go.'

His main concern is pollution in China. 'Japan is very close to China geographically and we have so much Chinese stuff in Japan.' He believes he can make a difference by buying more domestic products.

In terms of trade-offs he says, 'I ride my bike to the office, so I cannot have train money paid. I'm doing right and good but am disadvantaged. It's unfair. Riding a bike is part of my life so I give up about $100 per month.'

Sugito is not prepared to compromise on good quality or design to choose the greener choice: 'Eco is not my first priority... though I know I should care more about eco.' He is also not prepared to give up travelling abroad: 'You need to go outside to see your own country objectively.'

My world: Ash, the young Singapore journalist

Ash is a single 19-year-old freelance journalist and student living in Singapore.

He recycles all the magazines and newspapers he accumulates. 'I tear out the sheets to use as wrapping paper and notebook covers. I don't print any of my documents either, to save paper.' But he feels he could be doing more: 'Currently, I make the effort to only retrieve all my scrap paper to give them a second life because as a writer, they have sentimental value to me. I'd like to be able to do the same for the rest.'

Ash takes public transport everywhere, buys organic, local and fair-trade produce and feels very strongly about the fair treatment of workers. 'Having visited a village in Jakarta [Indonesia] that practised 'fair trade' … [it] widely broadened my perception on the issue. It's a lot more important for people to see that being green also helps our society.'

He believes everyone can support fair trade by ensuring people are paid a sustainable wage. 'I can make a difference by volunteering to run background checks on the organization that is paying them.'

Ash finds that buying organic products in Singapore comes at a cost: 'Organic food or even organic clothing is a lot more expensive… there is a "special" rack for [organic cotton clothing] at the shop I go to. No one ever goes there because it's "green", and thus inevitably expensive. So the compromise is definitely the cost factor.' But it also brings its own reward: 'When [you] actually wear something organic, you feel special and different.'

He finds that government action in Singapore appears well meant but is ineffective: 'It seems to be all talk and no action… If they really wanted to make an effort, they'd attempt to promote sustainable living every day instead of doing it on an event basis (Earth Day, Earth Conservation Day). It seems superficial.'

Ash believes business can do more by offering corporate support and sponsorships to events that promote sustainable living. He has found that although many brands test the green market in Singapore, they pull out when they find it doesn't seem to resonate with their target audience. 'They treat eco as a fad – particularly in fashion. They fail to understand that this is not a "current trend" but a lifestyle.'

Ash started the RecycloFashion PR and Communications agency to express a professional interest in the 'alternative'. 'Now, it's starting to get a lot personal on our part. We want people to understand that there are choices they can make that are good and make them stand out from others as well.'

My world: Summerly, the London art gallery owner

Summerly is 31 years old. She lives in West London with her partner and 'free range' little boy of 20 months, and her interest in green issues is both professional and personal. As the operations director of notonthehighstreet.com, Summerly's work is focused on developing and supporting small UK-based business that offer British-made or locally produced goods. 'Few of our partners use warehouses, instead working from home or local workshops, and many reuse and recycle packaging for dispatch.'

As a mother, she feels strongly about feeding her family organic food. 'I do question the quality of meat and vegetables that are not organic.' She buys her food locally and shops seasonally, visiting a local farmer's market and receiving a regular home delivery of vegetables, although she is aware that this may have cost implications.

'However, all food costs do seem to be going up, so I'm not even sure if the equivalent shop at a supermarket would be significantly more expensive.'

Summerly would like to use different nappies and wipes for her son, but feels the compromise in quality is not worth it: 'He seems happier (and stays dry) in Huggies! There is also a cost implication; organic nappies/wipes cost an absolute fortune.'

She recycles weekly – 'The council now provides all sorts of different-coloured bags and boxes' – and although she feels guilty even saying it, finds the task of sorting the rubbish very time consuming: 'Our recycling does seem to take hours now!'

It would be difficult to compromise on overseas travel as she has family abroad. 'We often plan to travel by train to Europe; however, the cost is not competitive.'

Summerly is cynical of the government's motives in introducing so-called 'green' measures that are simply stealth taxes. 'Has the congestion charge had a real impact on the environment?' And she sees businesses as having a responsibility to promote sustainability both operationally and in the products and services they provide.

4 Conscience consumers

- How to understand what matters to conscious consumers.
- How to segment consumers by their engagement level.
- How to collaborate with consumers to do more.

The logic for putting sustainability at the heart of your business strategy does not come from governments or environmentalists, but from consumers themselves. Market research shows a steady growth in demand for responsible products and services, bought from companies with responsible sourcing and distribution.

Consumers increasingly think and act more consciously. The majority of people – from Bangkok to Boston, Copenhagen to Cape Town – say that social and environmental factors affect their purchase choices, even in economically tough times. Across the world, 79 per cent say it matters (GfK Group), and 64 per cent say they would pay a premium (TNS Global). On average they would be prepared to pay a premium of 11 per cent (Accenture). Interestingly, all of these figures are higher in developing than in developed markets.

The leader of the confectionery giant who once stated he would never reduce the amount of packaging on his chocolates because his competitors were 'unlikely to do the same' has seen his consumers migrate to companies that have been bolder. The airline leader who used to claim that his passengers weren't concerned about carbon emissions has now invested billions in a new fleet of cleaner aircraft, and can't stop telling those same passengers about it.

Segmenting your consumers based on their responsible attitudes is a useful step in being able to target more responsible propositions. People can be grouped in general attitudinal groups, using indicators such as their attitudes (by researching their principles and priorities) and behaviours (do they recycle, choose fair-trade food, give to charity, do voluntary work?), and then evaluated in terms of potential to engage them profitably.

However, more important than products themselves – and the way they are sourced and produced, sold and disposed of – is to address the way people use them.

Helping people to be good

In his book, *Hot, Flat, and Crowded*, Thomas Friedman describes one of the biggest challenges to sustainability as being 'affluenza'. It is a term used by the critics of consumerism. Wikipedia describes it as 'a painful, contagious, socially transmitted condition of overload, debt, anxiety and waste resulting from the dogged pursuit of more', whilst a competing entry calls it 'the bloated, sluggish and unfulfilling feeling that results from efforts to keep up with the Joneses'.

Whilst this is undoubtedly a regular condition on the streets of Manhattan's Fifth Avenue or London's Bond Street, it is also incredibly visible in the developing world. In the streets of East Europe the most common female accessories are a Louis Vuitton bag and glasses, whilst males prefer the BMW logo proudly embossed on their car keys. But it is also in the mind-boggling speed and scale of new cities such as Doha in Qatar and Dalian in China. There is no easy cure.

The 'Greendex' from National Geographical ranks people across nations by their attitudes to sustainability. It finds the highest proportions of consumers that embrace sustainable behaviours in Brazil, India and China; and the lowest levels in Japan, France, and, bottom of the list, the United States.

The analysis suggests that people in the first group of countries are less driven by image and guilt but instead embrace sustainable behaviours as a natural aspect of social fairness. They feel more afraid and responsible for their future, because they live in more threatened parts of the world, or think longer term. They are more willing to change, maybe because they have less to give up. However, they still aspire to improve themselves, and to achieve better lifestyles, and so need guidance in achieving that sustainably. There is hope in the emerging world.

So where do we start? Do consumers really want to live better?

Today's consumers are more powerful, demanding and informed than ever. They are also more emotional and intuitive. They will love you or hate you. And tell the world. They want positive choices, not trade-offs or compromises.

People typically have good intentions, but need help to do the right thing. They know that some foods are healthier than others, but are confused by antioxidants and unsaturated fats (are they good or bad?). They know that recycling is sensible, but can never remember which of the four coloured boxes to put what in (and sometimes wonder if it really matters). They know that the 4×4 station wagon is not good for the environment, but have a tribe of kids who need transporting around (with all their gear too).

Strategically you then need to choose whether to favour the 'good' consumers. If they also happen to be the most profitable audiences, then it's a no-brainer. But if not, you need to consider how you can have a profitable relationship with them. Should you continue to support all groups, or be selective? Editing becomes important, either by helping consumers to make more informed choices, or by pre-selecting the better solutions for them.

More philosophical is the question of your relationship with these 'wonderful people' you call consumers. Are they just numbers and transactions or are they something more? A more sustainable approach might be to think of them as partners, sharing in the purpose you have set yourself – and together making the world a better place. As a result, they care more, will do more for you, stay with you and engage others.

Good growth requires a more interdependent relationship with your market, doing good as a business, and enabling consumers to do even more good themselves.

Enabling people to be good

Whilst most consumers are aware of at least some of the social and environmental challenges in today's world, many do connect this with their everyday behaviours, the lifestyles they seek to lead, the purchase decisions they make.

Sustainability issues might be essential to the survival of Planet Earth, but to most consumers they are still optional. Whilst governments and lobby groups might insist we have no option (and indeed, we might not), consumers will only do things that they want to do. Whilst this 'pull, not push' approach might seem soft, it is more likely to engage people, more likely to deliver sustained behaviour change and to succeed.

You can't tell people to be good, but you can encourage them to want to be.

Whilst they may well have a 'conscience' in some respects – exhibited, for example, by their healthy eating or recycling, doing voluntary work or offsetting air travel – they might not be consistent in everything they do.

There are many reasons why consumers seek to do 'the right thing' but fail. These might be, for example, because of a lack of understanding about how things connect (how does air conditioning connect with pictures of melting ice caps?), or because of a trade-off they are not ready or able to make (they know 4×4 SUVs are not good, but still have four kids to transport around), or because of a confusion about what is the better choice (to support the flower growers of Kenya or avoid the overuse of precious water and unnecessary impacts of transportation by buying locally?).

Enabling and energizing

'Conscience' is a state of mind, an emotional driver, often irrational and intuitive. If we think back to Maslow's hierarchy of needs – from the basic needs of survival up to the more esoteric needs of 'self-actualization' – then we could more simply define these needs as essential to non-essential, from rational to emotional, from helping people to exist to enabling people to achieve more.

The motivations of consumers could therefore be more simply ordered into three types:

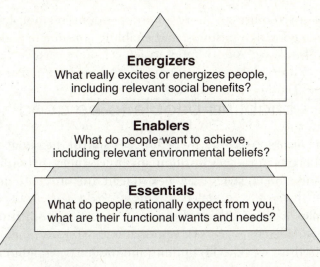

Figure 4.1 Energizer pyramids reflect the rational and emotional motives of consumers and how to develop business responses at each level (source: Genius Works)

- *Essentials:* what they need and expect from you (the more conventional aspects of your products and services, and basic sustainable practices they would expect from any company today).
- *Enablers:* what they would like to achieve as a result (these are typically fairly rational factors, and include enabling them to live or work in a more environmentally supportive way).
- *Energizers:* what inspires them, sparks their imagination (these are more emotional factors, traditionally small added-value gestures, but also including the more social, human aspects of sustainability).

Most businesses focus on the essentials. They offer basic products, meeting the essential needs and wants of consumers. As a result, their rational products are bought in rational transactions and are increasingly reduced to low-margin commodities in the eyes of consumers.

A more enlightened approach is to focus on enablers and energizers.

As an enabler rather than a mere supplier, the business focuses more on helping consumers to achieve their real goals, applying products and increasingly services to form relevant solutions. The business becomes more important to them. They energize and inspire people by the extra things they do, or enable people to do for themselves, things they tell their friends about. They focus not just on what people do and how they do it, but how they feel too. This is a much more emotional approach that builds engagement, trust and loyalty.

Achieving more

Sustainability issues are opportunities to achieve more – whilst most products and services address the 'essentials', social and environmental benefits are more 'enabling' and even 'energizing'.

Oxfam, the charity that supports social issues in Africa, developed a fantastic programme called 'Oxfam Unwrapped'. Stuck for a present to buy someone who has everything? Buy them a donkey that is donated to a family in Africa. Or a cow, a water-purification kit, or even a new school. Concerned about the number of trees required to make all the cards you send at Christmas? Explain that you've donated the money to Africa, and a family got a chicken instead of your friends getting their card. Happy Christmas!

But sustainable issues have to be relevant to the consumer, as do the benefits that they deliver – just as fashions are incredibly personal. A fashion that is energizing to one person is not to another. It's about matching the right issues with the right person.

This requires that we understand people more deeply. We explore their needs beyond the narrow parameters of functional specifications of products. We need to start learning about consumers more holistically, about what they use products for and how they use them, and more about their general motivations and aspirations in life.

Deep diving

One way to achieve this is through a deep 'immersion' approach to consumer research.

Companies are increasingly rejecting the standard quantitative forms of research – questionnaires, focus groups and purchase tracking – to get down 'deep and dirty' with consumers. Spend time talking to them – about them, what they do and what they dream. Go shopping with them, spend time with them and their family, watch them work, watch them shop. Through this approach we build a much better picture of what they seek. We begin to understand their psyche, their values, their conscience.

Some organizations send their managers out on consumer 'missions', to do things that consumers do, at least once a week. This is not just being a mystery shopper, but more fundamentally being a consumer – with the same hassles of parking the car, hunting the supermarket aisles, waiting in queues, finding somewhere to store what you've bought and dispose of it sometime later. Other organizations, for example when entering a new market, send managers to live with consumers for weeks and even months.

As a result, you learn about real people, real lives and real opportunities. The problem with data analysis is that the most emotional, personal and the more emerging issues like aspects of sustainability get averaged out. We end up focusing on the essentials of the masses. We never learn from the more thoughtful person, the more important people and the things that will matter most in the future.

The new consumer agenda

Conscience consumers have many different needs and wants, aspirations and priorities. However, when you immerse yourself deeper into the consumer's world, an interesting pattern begins to emerge. Some people are more personally motivated, others collectively, some parochial, and others by the changing world around them. We can categorize the different issues that matter most to people in the following groups:

- *Me.* These are personal issues, such as health, education and happiness.
- *My world.* These are local issues, such as family and friends, local communities.
- *The world.* These are global issues, such as poverty, ethics and the environment.

Consumers tend to gravitate to one of these groups more than the others. All of the issues might matter, but some more than others. There is no good and bad. The group to which people find themselves closest is largely driven by influences such as their upbringing and family, travel and education:

- *'Me' people* tend to be young and single, more independent and establishing themselves in the world. They are also those parents whose children have left home and they feel they have their lives back again.
- *'My world'* people are typified by new parents and grandparents where children inspire a new level of conscience, caring about the world in which they will live. This is shared by people who live in strong, small communities where there is a spirit of collective support.
- *'The world'* people are more religious and intellectual. They may well have travelled widely and campaign more actively for global causes. They are fewer in number but tend to be the most vocal.

Of course, these are (dangerous) generalizations, and it is impossible to label people in such simple ways. However, the groupings are useful anchors around which to develop propositions that will more effectively engage different people.

Beyond green

What is interesting is that most green initiatives address 'the world' issues, and so the vast majority of people have only a secondary engagement in them. Companies would be much better off addressing more relevant issues, or at least using the more relevant issues as a bridge to others.

Consumers don't see social and environmental issues in isolation from other issues. They want a great-tasting meal as well as one that has been sustainably sourced. They want a fast car as well as one with low emissions. They like the idea of organic clothing but not if loses its shape and doesn't feel great to wear.

Focusing on benefits rather than features is important too. Locally sourced food is often fresher and tastier, as well as supporting local economies and involving fewer transport emissions. Think about what matters most to the consumer. Buying second-hand clothes rather than new ones obviously reduces incredible amounts of production emissions and materials, and the clothing can be presented as 'vintage' rather than 'used' – more positive and cool.

Segmenting the conscience consumers

There are many ways to categorize consumers and to segment markets. Whilst it is relatively easy to define consumers in terms of demographics – age, sex, income and location – it is much harder to define them in terms of their motivations – attitudes, influences, behaviours and intentions. Yet in a connected, emotional world these latter factors become much more important. Two physically similar people are unlikely to share many of the same experiences and attitudes.

There is no definitive way to categorize or segment the different levels of attitude and behaviour amongst 'conscience' consumers.

Each research company typically develops its own definitions and therefore segments. Some recent examples are shown below (where, for comparison, the percentages relate to proportions of the US adult population).

'LOHAS' (Lifestyles of Health and Sustainability) is a term used by a number of research firms to indicate people who pursue 'good' lifestyles – organic and healthy food, household-waste recycling, environmentally friendly cleaning products, alternative healthcare, fitness and wellbeing.

Landor Green Brands 2007	Hartman Adaptive Reactions 2007	Yankelovich Going Green 2007	LOHAS Consumer Trends 2008
Bright greens (engaged, demand) 34%	Radical engagement (people together) 36%	Greenthusiasts (high attitude/ high behaviour) 13%	LOHAS (do all they can) 17%
Green motivated (accept and do some) 10%	Sustained optimism (rely on science) 27%	Greenspeaks (high attitude/ low behaviour) 15%	Naturalites (do personal things) 17%
Green hypocrites (aware but don't do) 26%	Divine faith (leave it to God) 20%	Greensteps (medium attitude/medium behaviour) 25%	Drifters (do it for image) 24%
Green ignorants (unengaged) 19%	Cynical pessimism (we have no chance) 9%	Greenbits (low attitude/ high behaviour) 19%	Conventionals (do practical things) 26%
Dull greens (don't care) 11%	Pragmatic acceptance (don't worry about it) 8%	Greenless (low attitude/low behaviour) 29%	Unconcerned (don't do it) 16%

Sources: landor.com, hartman-group.com, yankelovich.com, nmisolutions.com

The LOHAS network claims that in the United States this represents around 16 per cent of the adult population and represents $209 billion in consumer sales (based on 2005 data).

A more detailed approach comes from Blue Sky, a sustainability research firm that specializes in segmentation of markets. It categorizes consumers in shades of green:

- **Dark greens**: idealists, the more committed ethical consumer; the market conscience. They demand more rigour, higher standards, detailed information. They grow their own vegetables, flying is not an option as carbon must be cut, not offset.
- **Bright greens**: pragmatists, interested in positive choice and easy action, ie prepared to make small changes, but not radical shifts, in behaviour.

They want brands and retailers to choose ethically on their behalf. They buy seasonal local food, walk the children to school, consider going by train to European holiday destination, yet their savings are with the bank that offers the most competitive rates.

- **Light greens**: the ordinary consumers (mainstream market) who have simply added ethical responsibility to the matrix of decision making. They look for win-win situations, ie enhanced lifestyle benefits of using products that are more ethical, eg smart new technologies and ways to save money while cutting emissions. They recycle, turn the lights off, but keep the heating on high, are interested in responsible travel but take a long-distance flight to get there.

- **Pale greens**: they suffer from eco-anxiety and feel defeatist in the face of the huge, overwhelming problems associated with global warming: 'What can I do about it?' They may still adopt some eco-friendly behaviours – hence they appear on the sliding scale of greenness – but this is likely to be motivated purely by self-interest, eg 'I choose organic (food/clothes/cosmetics) because it's/they're good for me.'

Green Sky Thinking, a brand planning partnership, believes that people tend to shift up and down this sliding scale of greenness according to personal priorities, benefits, lifestyle choice, life stage and influences. They make constant trade-offs and as a result show no consistency in their ethical remit, eg they recycle diligently, cycle, buy fair trade or local, but use disposable nappies and buy blueberries flown in from Argentina because they're this year's 'super food'.

Perhaps the most intuitive segmentation model comes from Joel Makower in his book, *Strategies for the Green Economy*, where he reflects on the different approaches to segmentation and prefers to focus less on awareness or concern for the issues, more on knowing what to do about it, and doing it. He defines five (it's always five!) kinds of 'good' consumer:

- Committed: knows what to do and does it often.
- Conflicted: knows what to do but often doesn't bother.
- Concerned: wants to know what to do but doesn't yet.
- Confused: doesn't know what to do or how to make a difference.
- Cynical: doesn't know and doesn't care.

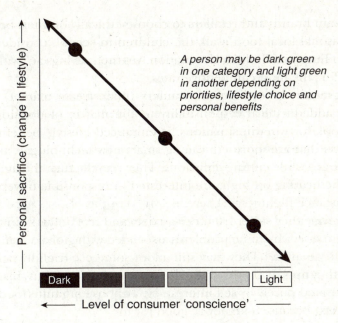

A person may be dark green in one category and light green in another depending on priorities, lifestyle choice and personal benefits

Figure 4.2 Levels of conscience: there are many ways to interpret the attitudes and behaviours of consumers (source: Green Sky Thinking)

Coca-Cola and Danone: seeing a different side of life

Coca-Cola and Danone both produce a range of food and drink products, although the former concentrates primarily on carbonated drinks whilst the latter specializes mainly in dairy products and bottled water. Whilst Coca-Cola is just beginning to move beyond corporate communications into eco-efficiency and recycling, Danone's more advanced approach is beginning to embed sustainability in its commercial operations, experimenting with new business models and value-chain structures.

Coke's challenges

The Coca-Cola Company is the world's largest beverage company, with a portfolio of nearly 400 brands and a logo that ranks amongst the most recognized icons in the world. Coke products are drunk by people from all sectors of society in almost every country in the world. A Coca-Cola product is consumed 1.5 billion times every day. Coca-Cola therefore has enormous direct and indirect impacts on the environment, health and society. Coca-Cola's economic success also trickles down to communities: a study conducted in South Africa estimated that, for every job created by the Coca-Cola system, an additional 16 jobs are created indirectly.

The production of Coca-Cola depends on three main commodities: sugar, aluminium and water. Sugar, of which the world produces around 140 million tonnes per year, is regarded as one of the most damaging of all crops, both because of the amount of land required to grow it and because of the impacts of intensive cultivation on wildlife habitats; an estimated 5 to 6 million hectares of cropland are lost each year due to soil erosion and degradation, according to WWF. Sugar cultivation and refining also require enormous amounts of water – around 200 litres for a single can of cola, WWF claims, on top of the one to three litres per can used directly to make and dilute the syrup base. Open-cast bauxite mining – the source of the aluminium used to make drinks cans – destroys wildlife habitats and can cause a range of environmental problems, such as soil degradation, noise pollution, atmospheric dust and cadmium contamination.

Waste is also a challenge; US citizens alone send around 36 billion aluminium cans to landfill each year, despite an estimated scrap value of $600 million, and only 10 per cent of Coke's plastic bottles are currently recycled, according to corporate sustainability newsletter *Environmental Leader*.

Finally, Coca-Cola's products have been accused of fuelling obesity (one can of Coca-Cola contains approximately 10 teaspoons of sugar) and offering little nutritional value.

The key challenges for Coca-Cola therefore are: to reduce the environmental impacts of aluminium and sugar production; to reduce the business's demand on water supplies; to bring about higher rates of recycling; and to tackle challenges related to obesity and nutrition. Coca-Cola also needs to manage the transport-based carbon emissions of its distribution network, since its liquid products are relatively heavy and often transported over long distances.

Coke's response

Coke's approach to sustainability focuses on four areas: active lifestyles; climate and energy protection; water stewardship; and sustainable packaging. Coke has pledged to:

- 'Refresh the world in body, mind and spirit by anticipating our consumers' desires and needs;
- 'Provide great jobs and protect the workplace rights of all our associates;

- 'Replace every drop of water we use;
- 'Design packaging that will be seen as a valuable resource for future use;
- 'Grow our business but not our carbon footprint;
- 'Help to improve the wellbeing of the people in the communities where we operate.'

In January 2007, Coke launched a global Workplace Rights Policy, which was guided by the United Nations International Labor Organization (ILO) principles and other human rights organizations. Coke's Workplace Rights Policy formalizes its long-standing commitment to ensuring that each one of its approximately 71,000 associates around the world is treated fairly and with dignity. Through the UN Global Compact, Coke agrees to 'embrace, support and enact' a set of core values in the areas of human rights, labour standards, the environment and anti-corruption. (Many of its bottling partners are also signatories to the UN Global Compact.)

Most recently, Coke announced the launch of a new subsidiary, Coca-Cola Recycling LLC (CCR), to recycle packaging for reuse within Coke's North American operations. CCR has grand ambitions: to build 'the world's largest plastic bottle recycling plant', to reuse 100 per cent of its packaging, and to work with the United States National Recycling Coalition to develop ways of recycling PET, aluminium, cardboard and plastics. Coke has also announced plans for a new bottle design that is wholly recyclable and uses 5 per cent less PET than the traditional bottle.

Coke is also working with consumer groups and non-profit organizations to enable and encourage consumers to return containers for reuse and recycling, rather than throwing them away.

Danone's challenges

Groupe Danone (known as Dannon in the United States) is a food-product company headquartered in France. It is the world leader in the manufacture and marketing of dairy products and bottled water, and, following the acquisition of Numico in 2007, the second-largest producer of baby foods.

Amongst its portfolio of brands are Danone/Dannon yogurts and several brands of bottled water including Volvic, Evian and Badoit. In Asia, it owns Yili, Aqua and Robust, as well as 51 per cent of China's Wahaha joint-venture company, giving it a total market share of 20 per cent and making it the leading vendor of packaged water in Asia. About 56 per cent of its 2006 net sales derived from dairy, 28 per cent from beverages, and 16 per cent from biscuits and cereals.

Besides its economic contribution, Danone believes that its most important impacts lie in the area of nutrition; its corporate mission is 'to provide healthy food for as many people as possible'.

It too has significant impacts on the environment, especially in terms of greenhouse gases: methane (from cows) is a more powerful greenhouse gas than carbon dioxide; nitrogen fertilizers used to grow fodder are manufactured from fossil fuels; water and dairy products are relatively heavy, resulting in significant carbon emissions from their transport to retail and then to people's homes; and land that is used for grazing is not available for (and has sometimes been cleared of) trees. Thanks to this combination of factors, WWF say that dairy products have one of the highest 'environmental footprints' of any foods.

Danone's key challenges therefore include the provision of healthy, nutritious products and the mitigation of greenhouse gas emissions (particularly methane).

Danone's response

In support of its mission to provide healthy food, the Danone Institute International awards a biennial prize worth €120,000 to individuals or teams that have advanced the science of human nutrition. Past winners include: Jeffrey Friedman, who revealed the role of genes in regulating body weight; David Barker, for his hypothesis that under-nutrition in the womb can lead to coronary heart disease later in life; and Ricardo Bressani, for his work fighting undernourishment in South America.

According to Danone, its strong focus on nutrition is couched in the context of a healthy respect for nature and human development. In 2007, Danone launched a new initiative called Way Ahead, based on two pillars: respect for five 'fundamentals' – human rights, human relations, the environment, the consumer and corporate governance – and social innovation. Most of Danone's dairy and water products have now been assessed against the five fundamental criteria, and each subsidiary has embarked on projects to develop or consolidate economic activity that enriches the local community and engages employees.

Since 1996, Danone has been working to its own 'environmental charter' that set industrial and packaging targets to 2010. However, these outdated targets are expected to be met by 2008, so Danone is acquiring new tools and organizations capable of updating them and making them more stretching. Key amongst these will be reductions in carbon-dioxide emissions and water consumption throughout the value chain.

The impact

Despite recent commitments to adopt a leadership position on environmental responsibility (particularly with relation to water and packaging) Coke's performance so far has been modest. Coke has improved its energy efficiency by 16 per cent since 2002, and reduced its per-unit carbon footprint by means of energy-efficient, hydrofluorocarbon (HFC)-free vending machines and coolers. However, overall carbon-dioxide emissions continue to rise because of strong sales growth, and the level of recycling or reuse of solid waste remains roughly static.

Coke's stated goal of recycling or reusing all of its plastic bottles depends upon the success of new projects that will take some considerable time to bear fruit; how long is not clear, since no target date has been set.

People, planet, profit: the reality of consumers

The third button for consumers

Dan Esty sees sustainability as a 'third button' for consumers in their decision making. 'One of the key findings in the research underlying my *Green to Gold* book was that the number of consumers willing to buy on environmental criteria was quite limited. Customers care first and foremost about price and quality/performance. We argued that green factors could be the "third button" on which marketers focused.'

This situation is changing somewhat, he believes. 'There are now a number of markets where green consumers are an important force. The number of people willing to pay a premium for environmentally superior products seems to be rising, at least in some categories. For example, organic food is booming. The price premium paid for organic milk or other organic products is substantial.

'Customers care most about the price and the quality or performance of the goods that they are buying. There are, however, some subsets of the population that care a good bit about environmental factors. But customers are generally not willing to trade off the things they care most about for improved environmental performance.'

He gives the example of the early fluorescent lights that were both expensive and cast a somewhat odd greenish glow, and which were unsuccessful. Customers found it unacceptable to trade off the quality of the light and price for a superior environmental product.

'In general, I think the best strategy for businesses is to offer the customers choice. There is some segment of almost every marketplace where there are people willing to pay a premium for an environmentally superior product. Offering this segment of the consuming public a green option makes good business sense.'

Having a conscience in a digital world

Aegis sees a broader approach to consumer insight as the starting point of better engagement. 'Social and ethical issues are forming part of the purchase-decision model for many consumers. However, [the model] differs in nature and importance by sector and segment, depending upon the direct impact of certain goods and services.'

One key factor driving the growth in consciousness of green issues and their active inclusion in customer purchase decisions, believes Aegis's Nigel Morris, is the transparency of information created by the web.

'The use of search engines and social media to check not only on product characteristics but also the values, actions and behaviour of the companies that own these products and services is one of the biggest challenges facing brands in today's markets. This will only become more pronounced.'

Fairtrade, the symbol that needs no words

Over the past 15 years, customers have become increasingly aware of Fairtrade and increasingly supportive, showing their willingness to play their part in tackling poverty.

Recent TNS research shows that 70 per cent of the UK population recognize the Fairtrade mark, with 64 per cent of the population linking the mark to a better deal for producers in the developing world. This means the message of Fairtrade is getting through, as the research also shows that one in four of the UK's shoppers now regularly buys products carrying the mark.

The growing public awareness of Fairtrade is translating into increased purchasing, with a 72 per cent increase in sales in 2007. The Fairtrade Foundation attributes these leaps in sales and awareness of Fairtrade to the vibrant grassroots social movement.

Across the UK, there are now more than 350 Fairtrade towns, 4,000 Fairtrade churches, 37 Fairtrade synagogues, 60 Fairtrade universities and thousands of Fairtrade schools, all campaigning to support and promote Fairtrade in their local area.

5 Sustainable innovation

- How to drive innovation as a way of turning problems into opportunities.
- How to find the best opportunities for streamlining and enhancing.
- How to embrace social entrepreneurship in your business.

A cup of instant coffee takes 1,000 cups of water to make.

A bunch of fair-trade flowers from Kenya consumes water equivalent to that needed by 100 people, and requires more kerosene than a transatlantic flight. A nice idea to support African farmers develop their livelihoods, but at unbelievable social and environmental cost.

There are 4,100 litres of water embedded in a single cotton T-shirt.

There must be a better way.

As the global population explodes from 6.5 billion to 9 billion by 2050, by which date the scientists demand an 85 per cent global reduction in carbon emissions compared to today, we aspire to ever better lifestyles. We live longer, with a boom in global travel at lower cost enjoyed by many more people. We experience exotic foods and seek to import more of them. We smile at the summer sunshine but not as it sparks droughts and rationing.

Is this situation sustainable? Can we have the best of both worlds?

We look to innovation as the magical answer: cleaner sources of energy that don't pollute our skies, faster communications that reduce our need to travel, biotechnologies that improve our health and wellbeing, ethical finance that doesn't support corrupt regimes.

Consider an alternative scenario where sustainable innovation is not about compromise. The latest sports cars from Tesla combine lowest emissions with the fastest speeds. The (RED) clothing venture, championed by rock star Bono and partnering with the likes of Apple and Armani, is able to combine 'cool' consumption with relieving HIV/AIDS in Africa. The Ethiopian fair-trade coffee in Starbucks supports local farmers with fair prices and conditions, and tastes great too.

Of course, there is also a role for needing, buying and using less – reducing the non-essentials – the unnecessary travel, the frivolous cardboard packaging, the outdated manufacturing processes, the non-collaborative retailers, the mountains of waste.

The point is that sustainable innovation is rarely incremental, it is radical and disruptive, finding solutions to complicated problems and dilemmas that people face.

It considers total systems – from sourcing and production to consumption and renewal. It affects the whole business, often being less about what the product is, more about how it is made and used. And it can change the game, the basis of competition, the source of differentiation, the nature of consumption.

Innovation from the bottom up

Perhaps most exciting is the rise of 'social entrepreneurship': as investors begin to see the long-term profit potential of more sustainable innovations, they turn from Silicon Valley to invest in the start-up businesses that seek to grow by doing good.

These are rarely found in the big corporations or developed markets. They tend to be found on the fringes, smaller companies often in emerging markets. They represent the new flow of innovation from the bottom up, rather than top down.

Mohammad Yunas, the Nobel Prize winner and champion of microcredits is perhaps the most famous social entrepreneur, creating a system of small loans that enables many more people to start to live and work, spend and save in a more structured and lasting way.

Many socially entrepreneurial businesses already exist around the world – the marathon world record holder from Ethiopia who invests his winnings in building schools and hospitals in Addis Ababa, the Indian fabric manufacturer that uses non-polluting dyes to colour the cloth most in demand by the world's fashion design houses, and the South African home ware business where everything is sourced from scrap.

From Clinton and Blair to Gates and Buffett, everybody wants to do their bit. Although as Gates himself said, governments and large business need a fresh injection of ideas. They need to see things differently – from the developing world, the bottom of the pyramid, through the eyes of those who live in fear of drought, hunger and war.

Shokti Doi is a new brand of yogurt in Bangladesh. The name translates from Bengali as 'yogurt for power'. Grameen Danone Foods was set up as a joint venture between Nobel Prize winner Mohammad Yunus and French yogurt maker Danone to bring affordable nutrition to malnourished children in Bangladesh with a fortified yogurt. The venture kicked off in late 2005, when Franck Riboud, the CEO of Groupe Danone, took Yunus to lunch in Paris. 'We would like to find ways to help feed the poor,' said Riboud. The Indian entrepreneur, most famous for his Grameen Bank, suggested that they set up a hybrid between non-profit and for-profit.

Like a conventional business, Grameen Danone must break even. Yet, like a non-profit operation, it is driven by a purpose rather than by profit. If it grows profitably, then investors receive a small reward, a 1 per cent dividend, with 99 per cent of profits being ploughed back into the venture. The first factory was deliberately small, as a prototype and symbol for community-based plants that would provide jobs across Bangladesh, encouraging many local entrepreneurs to establish their own plants, spreading the benefits more widely. 'Whilst we make money, we can also do good,' Riboud says.

With new sources of capital, combined with the right strategies and processes, global production and distribution partners, these businesses have a crucial role to play in creating a more balanced economy and more balanced world.

Social and environmental drivers of innovation

The best innovations respond to consumers, to their needs and aspirations. They address the possibilities delivered by emerging markets, or the vacant space where markets overlap.

Innovations might harness new technologies, new science, new ideas – or they might just use existing capabilities structured in a different way – a new design, application or business model for making or selling it.

Social and environmental issues are the fastest-emerging motivations for consumers today – both in existing markets (improving existing products, addressing existing consumers), and in new markets (creating new products, for new consumers):

- **Improving existing markets**: carbon-efficient vehicles, biodegradable packaging and organically nutritious foods.
- **Creating new markets**: video conferencing as an alternative to air travel, genetically modified crops or natural medicines.

Sustainable issues are therefore the biggest catalysts for innovation in business today – the best opportunities to create new sources of competitive advantage and new drivers of profitable growth.

However, sustainability is inherently about trade-offs. Call them choices, compromises or sacrifices, but by bringing a new set of agendas to the fore, we have more complexity than ever before. Whilst sometimes it is possible to overcome the sacrifice, or make a 'brilliant' compromise, most of the time we struggle to choose the lesser of two evils.

This is where innovation can be most powerful and beneficial. Resolving these trade-offs offers business growth and new opportunities for competitive differentiation.

Examples of different types of consumer trade-offs include:

Sustainability	**Functionality**
Should I buy a smaller car with lower carbon emissions?	Or should I buy a larger car with space for all the family
Functionality	**Functionality**
Should I buy a larger car with space for all the family?	Or should I buy a sports car that I've always dreamed of?
Sustainability	**Sustainability**
Should I buy a lighter car just imported from Asia?	Or should I buy a second-hand car from a local retailer?

Examples of different types of business trade-offs include:

Sustainability	**Functionality**
Should I source materials from the most environmentally friendly supplier?	Or should I source materials from the highest-quality supplier?
Functionality	**Functionality**
Should I source materials from the highest-quality supplier?	Or should I source materials from the lowest-price supplier?
Sustainability	**Sustainability**
Should I source materials from the most environmentally friendly supplier?	Or should I source materials from the most socially supportive supplier?

Whatever the catalyst or trade-off, the starting point for innovation is the market opportunity.

Mapping markets identifies where there is high growth or 'white spaces' of demand that are not being fulfilled, or the sectors and geographies where consumers are most ready for a more sustainable alternative. By focusing at a macro level on the best markets, you can then dive more deeply into the needs and motivations of existing and potential consumers in these markets.

Establishing some clear business objectives at this point is important, so as to give the innovation both direction and boundaries, typically something that helps the company to achieve its higher purpose in some more profitable and more sustainable way.

Innovation then becomes a disciplined yet creative process – one in which you 'open up' to explore as many possibilities as possible, and then 'close down' on the best in terms of their likely impact on consumers and business.

In fact there are three phases to sustainable innovation: explore, design and focus:

- **Discover**: opening up the possibilities, exploring as many ideas as possible, working with consumers and employees, learning from experts and other sectors, embracing new concepts, challenging conventions and stretching imaginations.
- **Design**: connecting the best ideas together to create stronger 'molecular' concepts, adding more sustainable elements to strengthen them. Challenging them to make them carbon neutral, more energy efficient or more socially positive.
- **Delivery**: closing down on the best concepts, as you shape them further. Evaluating which ones will most effectively achieve the purpose, drive most revenue and profit, at what cost and efficiency, in what time and with how much risk.

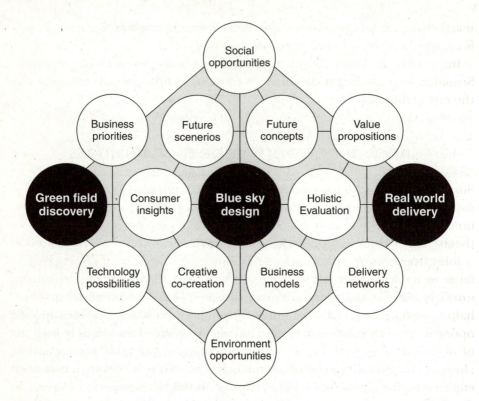

Figure 5.1 Sustainable innovation is a creative and commercial process, opening up, then closing down (source: Genius Works)

Whilst many companies feel they have enough ideas, or that 'a quick brainstorm' will suffice before getting on with focusing on a few ideas to make happen, the lack of diverse and significant ideas is often the biggest challenge. This is why so much innovation is incremental, not exciting, and quickly copied. You need to break out of conventions, challenge people to think more radically, to consider what is possible, not probable.

The second phase represents the all-important turning point from creative ideas into commercial innovations. As you progress you can challenge and improve concepts, improving their sustainability, as well as overall attractiveness. These 'creative fusions' are where the real innovations happen – often less about the product and more about the processes that support them, less about the business and more about the consumer.

Innovations emerge only in the third phase. This is where financial disciplines and practicality kick in – how much, how, and is it worth it? The most significant innovations typically embrace change to all aspects of a business – product, service, process and business model – but also change to the market – consumer application and behaviour, channels and pricing, how it is communicated and sold, stored or disposed of.

Innovation is about turning great ideas into commercial solutions. Sustainable innovations do this in a way that is also good for society and the environment.

Innovating every aspect of business

Sustainable innovations are emerging all around us. Consider these five stories of how experienced business leaders have embraced sustainability to innovate in different ways, by investing in others, setting up new businesses themselves or bringing together others to do so.

John Doerr is one of America's most famous venture capitalists. He rose to fame by spotting innovations that would have a disruptive impact on the world, betting on radical ideas like Amazon and Google. Now he's focused on halting global warming through innovation. He calls it 'the largest economic opportunity of the 21st century' and has already poured hundreds of millions of dollars into 'green' technology start-ups. From the mass production of cheap solar cells that can be rolled out on roofs, to plug-in hybrid automotive engines, biofuel from non-edible cellulose to the re-engineering of yeast so that it ferments sugars into fuel, he recognizes that these business face bigger challenges than online shopping and search engines, but that the impact could be even more significant, and the financial returns too.

On the cultured boulevards of France's capital city, the Velib self-service cycling scheme has been an extraordinary success. In its first 12 months of operation over 30 million rentals demonstrated the willingness of Parisians to adopt a greener form of transport. The scheme was set up by Jean-Charles Decaux, the CEO of outdoor advertising agency J C Decaux. Bikes are becoming big business for the €2-billion company, which is currently install-ing Velib schemes in over 50 cities around the world. Velib, which started in Vienna in 2005, is a subscription service, costing around €30 for one year's unlimited cycling.

Microsoft founder Bill Gates stepped down from the software giant in 2008 to devote his time and money to doing good. Whilst he has given away much of his wealth, around $29.7 billion to be precise, in recent years to support his favoured causes, he has also invested in many new ventures. His Cascade investment business includes a holding in Sapphire Energy, a California company that seeks to harness the potential of algae as motor fuel.

Mukesh Ambani, the Indian multi-billionaire, has great hopes for his Reliance Life Sciences business. It is testing intercropping of jatropha and pongamia – non-edible fuel crops that can grow on wasteland. It is also developing new hybrid varieties of seed that will double the biofuel yield in more irrigated environments. He is collaborating with Indian farmers to build clusters of 100,000 acres of crops that will support 100,000-tonnes biofuel extraction plants.

Larry Page and Sergey Brin, founders of Google, have a vision to make 'RE less than C', ie renewable energies cheaper than coal, and have a number of ventures with GE to address this challenge. They are major personal investors in Tesla Motors, which developed the Tesla Roadster electric vehicle, whilst Google has also invested $60 million to develop solar and wind power, plug-in hybrid cars and other ideas.

Even the sceptical Warren Buffett, commonly recognized as the world's greatest investor, is not slow in turning green. (He is sceptical because he is usually slow to embrace new technologies that he doesn't understand – such as web-based companies.) He is a major shareholder in MidAmerican Energy, a leading wind-energy company, and recently invested around $230 million in BYD, a Hong Kong-based producer of batteries for electric cars, which recently launched its first electric car, the e6.

Innovative at every level

Sustainable innovation can be applied at any level of the organization – from operational processes through to the way in which markets work, strategic and tactical, revolutionary or evolutionary:

1. *Process innovation*: improving efficiency, reducing waste – or more holistic-ally through redesign of value chains and the whole system of cradle to cradle;
2. *Product innovation*: new products and services that embrace new technical and sustainable dimensions as sources of differentiation;
3. *Market innovation*: addressing new needs and wants, finding new markets, whether new places for existing sectors, new sectors in existing places or both;
4. *Brand innovation*: developing a culture and identity that reflect the purpose and sustainable practices of the business;
5. *Business innovation*: rethinking the purpose of business, the business model by which it works, its stakeholders and measures of success;
6. *Strategic innovation*: changing the rules of the game by fundamentally changing how the business and its competitors work and compete.

Toyota, for example, uses its insights into the changing priorities of consumers to improve business efficiency as well as improving products and services. It focuses investments and resources on what matters most, and eliminates them from areas that matter less to consumers. This 'lean thinking' creates a natural responsiveness and efficiency across the whole business.

More generally we can apply these principles to any aspect of business by thinking about opportunities to streamline and elaborate:

- *'Streamlining'* is about reducing (or eliminating) aspects of business that are less important – typically finding cheaper, faster, lesser ways of achieving necessary evils. These might have a lower priority for consumers, or be a time-consuming chore for employees, or have a negative impact on society and the environment.
- *'Elaborating'* is about enhancing (or adding) aspects of business that are the most important – typically finding more engaging, more distinctive, more profitable ways of achieving these positive moments. These might have a high priority for consumers, or be an enjoyable or particularly rewarding aspect of work for employees, or be something that can have a more positive impact on society and the environment.

It is important to do both. Just as reducing costs is not a strategy for long-term success, sustainable compliance is not a route to greatness. It is about doing more, for more people, in innovative ways.

The creative potential of social entrepreneurs

Change the world. Make some money.

It's an appealing prospect. Non-profits were born because for-profits weren't addressing some market failures: pollution, poverty, illiteracy. Profit won't cure those ills but it's becoming a bigger part of more solutions.

Social entrepreneurs are individuals with innovative solutions to society's most pressing social problems. They are ambitious and passionate, addressing social issues either locally or globally, and offering new ideas for wide-scale change.

Instead of leaving society's needs to the government or big companies, social entrepreneurs find what is not working and solve the problem by changing the system, spreading the solution and persuading entire societies to take new leaps.

Many social entrepreneurs are natural communicators of their cause or idea – they recruit others, they engage partners, they find ways to overcome adversity, they make things happen that normal business procedures cannot. They are change makers.

Just as entrepreneurs change the face of business, so social entrepreneurs become the change agents of society, seizing opportunities others miss and improving systems, inventing new approaches and creating solutions to change society for the better. Whilst a conventional business entrepreneur might create entirely new industries, a social entrepreneur comes up with new solutions to social problems and then implements them on a large scale.

Whilst social entrepreneurs might seem to be separate from business, this need not be the case. Business can embrace social entrepreneurs – Bill Gates said we need them to inject more creativity, challenging received wisdom and providing new ideas. Small companies might find it easier than large ones to do this – or business can collaborate with social entrepreneurs, providing investment and resources, facilities and capabilities, to ensure that the best ideas have the most chance of making an impact.

There is also no reason why social entrepreneurs shouldn't make money at the same time as doing good. Even the most business-naive social entrepreneur can still find business partners with the expertise to help them to structure and develop their ideas, find finance and markets and make things happen in way that both achieves their social objectives and also has the potential to make significant money. This is the role of new social-innovation businesses such as Ashoka and Zoom Ventures. Many of the world's leading venture capitalists and investment funds, as well as mainstream businesses, are flocking to support social entrepreneurs too.

The social entrepreneurship market typically consists of many players, although one of its features is that it lacks ways of bringing the best people together:

1. *Social innovation*: using the catalyst of social problems as opportunities to do things differently, and the power of people and their ideas to create better solutions;
2. *Social entrepreneurs*: the individuals with the ambition and confidence to put themselves on the line, to set up their own business, to make their idea happen;
3. *Social ventures*: business start-ups designed to achieve a social purpose, either as a profit- or non-profit-making entity;
4. *Social investments*: investment funds ready to put their money into social ventures that will deliver the best return, typically measured over a longer term.

However, social entrepreneurship also needs help – particularly in developing markets where there is less education and there are fewer capabilities to turn ideas into reality:

1. ***Social capitalists***: businesses and individuals that are prepared to nurture and parent new start-ups, with access to resources, networks and know-how;
2. ***Ideas exchanges***: mechanisms that enable a budding social entrepreneur to present their idea to larger companies, and likewise for them to find entrepreneurs;
3. ***Innovation incubator***: support processes and facilities that help entrepreneurs shape, strengthen and speed their ideas to market;
4. ***Market networks***: distribution networks than enable entrepreneurs to reach new markets globally and enable larger companies to find and source them.

When C K Prahalad talks about the $5 trillion 'bottom of the pyramid' opportunity, he refers to the billions of people and the potential to support their growing aspirations and needs. It is social entrepreneurs, not large Western companies, that are most likely to succeed in these new markets.

That's what makes social entrepreneurship one of the most important and intriguing aspects of the new business world.

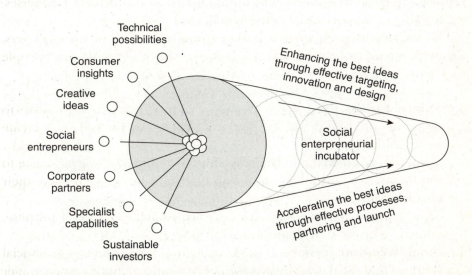

Figure 5.2 Social entrepreneurship: accelerating innovation through collaborative ventures focused on social and environmental issues (source: Zoom Ventures)

Amazon and eBay: redefining markets through innovation

Amazon and eBay are two giants of the internet revolution, jointly responsible for deep shifts in the way that consumers find, choose and consume a vast array of products and services. Unusually amongst leading companies, Amazon and eBay barely mention their attitudes, aspirations or performance in relation to environmental and social issues; and yet their impacts in both these areas go far beyond those of their peers in other industries.

Amazon's challenge

One of the iconic dot.com brands, US online retailer Amazon.com has expanded its business model in three important ways: territorially (with separate websites and operations in Canada, the UK, Germany, France, China and Japan); in the range of products sold (from books alone to DVDs, CDs, MP3 downloads, computer software, video games, electronics, apparel, furniture, food, toys and more); and in terms of its business model (from selling only its own products to acting also as a marketplace for other vendors).

Amazon's perseverance and emphasis on growth through technological innovation enabled it to survive when other internet start-ups failed (it turned its first profit in 2001, six years after its launch).

Innovation at Amazon is exercised with a disciplined focus on sales. Every page on the Amazon website is expected to contribute to sales in some way, usually by means of links to specific products. Moreover, Amazon's innovations have allowed for a sophisticated personal shopping experience that facilitates informed purchasing decisions. Features such as 'Search inside the book' give users access to the item's contents, while community features such as 'Listmania' and user reviews collectively provide a smooth and confidence-boosting online experience.

Amazon's success to date has challenged the existing paradigm of retail in several ways that minimize environmental impacts. First, it has removed the need for 'bricks and mortar' – buildings that require materials and energy to run, with their associated carbon emissions, waste, pollution and congestion. Second, it has created a direct link between the consumer and the warehouse, eliminating the need for distributing to stores large numbers of books that may remain unsold and need to be returned and pulped. Third, it has created a sense of community amongst consumers, who can swap reviews and recommendations about products. Next, it has encouraged the trade in used books, thereby limiting the demand for new ones; and its expansion into downloadable products (MP3s, software and so on) diverts some of its growth into a non-material form with lower environmental impacts.

However, Amazon also has significant negative environmental impacts. For example, its fierce dedication to sales growth tends to increase the demand for paper and other raw materials used to create its products; and the millions of servers, processors, computer screens and other electronic equipment used by both Amazon and its customers require large amounts of energy to run.

Amazon's challenge, therefore, is to use its famous powers of innovation to enable continued growth that does not have unacceptable environmental impacts.

Amazon's response

In 2007, Amazon.com launched Kindle, a 'wireless reading device' that can instantly download and display a book, newspaper or blog. Kindle can hold over 200 titles internally, and is easier to read than traditional monitors. Dubbed 'the iPod of ebooks' by the Sunday Times, the Kindle is expected to revolutionize the publishing industry in much in the same way that iPod and iTunes did the music industry.

eBay's challenge

eBay is the fastest-growing company in history. Having started life as a 'solution in search of a business model', it quickly expanded from a specialist site for enthusiastic amateur collectors to a multi-billion-dollar marketplace, with a leading presence in 37 countries. Once reserved for private individuals to sell to each other, around half of the products now traded on eBay are sold by businesses.

eBay's response

eBay's main contribution to sustainability has been to extend the useful lives of products that would otherwise have been discarded by their owners and either recycled, sent to landfill, incinerated or left as litter. Many might also have been traded offline, for example in car-boot sales, which themselves have some environmental impacts associated with transportation to and from site.

eBay's more recent acceptance of established retailers onto its marketplace has also removed some of the need for 'bricks and mortar' operations, such as retail outlets, with their associated greenhouse gas emissions, waste, pollution and nuisance.

The impact

eBay has spearheaded a social revolution, bringing together individuals from vastly different economic, social, cultural and geographic backgrounds in virtual communities of interest, and providing hundreds of thousands of people with the means to earn a living from home whilst fulfilling family and other commitments.

The benefits of Kindle for the environment are potentially huge and varied: it eliminates the need for paper, a major cause of deforestation, which is itself one of the most important drivers of climate change, soil degradation and water scarcity; it removes the need for inks and the energy and pollution linked with their production; it eliminates the huge amounts of post-consumer waste to be incinerated, sent to landfill or abandoned in public places; and (as long as it is durable, reliable and upgradeable) it need only be shipped once, whereas weighty books, magazine and newspapers must be packaged and transported continuously, causing further pollution and climate change.

There are also potential social benefits to Kindle. For example, it could remove barriers to entry for smaller publishers and authors by lowering production costs and giving easy access to customers, just as blogs and social networking sites did for the music industry.

So far, Kindle's success has been tremendous, despite subsequent competition from other electronic readers: within six months of its launch, Kindle was already taking 6 per cent of sales of books that were available in both hard copy and new electronic formats.

People, planet, profit: the reality of innovation

Nike develops a more Considered approach

Nike is exploring how brands can co-create more responsibly – with consumers, communities and entrepreneurs. Indeed, social entrepreneurship is a priority for the sportswear brand.

'We started working with Ashoka, who had an online competition called Changemakers, from which we developed our own online competition for social entrepreneurs – using sport for social change, which is a very niche area but also very engaging.'

The prize was small, symbolic really, a chance to come to the Nike campus and be trained by Nike marketing teams. It was an open-source competition, where people would submit their application openly online, enabling others to critique it. The response, despite no publicity, was unbelievable. Overnight Nike became a portal for entrepreneurs and consumers with a conscience.

'We think there is a shift in the model. We want to enable this incredible generation of entrepreneurs who are creating hybrids between a business and a social cause.' However, the key to a social venture is the ability to scale it to achieve its goals, efficiency and impact.

One of Nike's major focus areas is design. Mark Parker, CEO, is a designer, encouraging the business to see design as one of the big levers for everything it does. Nike have created the 'Considered' design team, which explores how to embrace sustainability for more responsible and better design. As Jones puts it, this is all about developing 'cradle-to-cradle products'.

Considered has become an ethos for the entire company. As Parker says, 'If all we do is create a green product line, then we've failed.'

Fashion as the great creative opportunity

'Fashion leads, it does not follow,' argues Dilys Williams from London College of Fashion. 'So it needs to drive business growth, and in today's world this means sustainable fashion. Young fashion designers who have innovative ideas for making fashion more sustainable are finding themselves in a very strong position in the marketplace. This is a very exciting time for new talent, new knowledge and new ideas. There are many new fashion start-ups due to increased demand, new sources of supply, access to markets achieved using new communication techniques, and the offer of an antidote to the "race to the bottom". There is a new confidence in design and it is questioning everything that we do and the ways in which we do it.

'We now have the greatest creative opportunity that we have seen in our lifetimes. There is a huge need for innovation that embraces sustainability in ways that people want, and that needs investment. This investment is attractive to all sizes of companies, as we have seen from Wal-Mart to graduate start-ups. It may be a long-term investment, but one with potentially great pay-offs to our future of our businesses.'

Finding new ways to love Unilever brands

Unilever has made sustainability a fundamental driver of brand innovation. 'Deepening the understanding of brands' impacts will become the predominant driver of innovation. But this needs to be done with real scientific rigour, predominantly through product design, and with true integrity not only in the way issues are tackled but also in the way we engage consumers in that conversation. Greenwash is becoming a real issue because it not only trivializes the whole problem but it also disempowers consumers by confusing them till exhaustion. Companies need to use marketing expertise not to get an irrelevant or confusing claim through but to help consumers get to grips with sustainable consumption and to encourage them to engage in a broader conversation with the brands they love, ruled by transparency.'

Of course, creating a product is only part of the story; how consumers use it invariably matters more. 'Most of fast-moving consumer goods company impacts are in consumer use of products. This is a reality. In the case of Unilever, approximately 86 per cent of our CO_2 emissions happen in consumer use of our products. So if we want to play our part in fighting climate change, we should not only speed up our eco-innovation agenda and influence regulations through advocacy but also start raising awareness with consumers about this issue and empowering them to make the right choices.'

Unilever believes that consumers generally want to do the right thing. 'They would love brands that address their impacts at every point. They want to know if by buying Lipton, for example, the growers of tea in East Africa will be treated in a fair way, that the environment will be respected and that the communities will benefit. Lipton's mission became to bring the grower and the drinker closer together, to make visible the wonderful power of East African communities and the environment that provides drinkers with a good product.'

Jonathon Porritt, the environmentalist working with Unilever on its Brand Imprint, describes this challenge as the utility–footprint correlation. In the end-of-abundance era, a new licence to use scarce resources could emerge. Restaurants in New York decided to discourage bottled water because in blind tests consumers perceived no difference between one brand and another. Consider the reduced impact of turning on the tap again, and saving on the many challenges of plastic bottles – an example that there is an embedded impact in everything we do.

New ways to innovate everything

Dan Esty at the Yale Center sees sustainability as one of the most important ways to generate innovation. 'A good number of businesses have found themselves stuck doing things the same way for a number of years. A focus on trying to solve environmental problems can help spur fresh thinking about ways to remake the company's goods or services so as to become solutions providers in response to problems like climate change, water availability, or the need to reduce chemical exposures in our society.'

He cites many examples where companies have used a green focus to help drive innovation. Toyota's desire for a 'car of the 21st century' that was much more energy-efficient and environmentally sound led not only to the development of the hybrid engine most famously deployed in the Prius, but also to innovations across the entire Toyota fleet. Now all Toyotas are much lighter than the competition due to advanced materials such as carbon fibre, and have 'smart systems' that improve the efficiency of the heating, air conditioning, 'and even the stereo'.

'Many companies are finding that it makes sense to launch a green line of products as a complement to their existing offerings in the marketplace. Clorox, for example, has developed a big new green line alongside its traditional chemical-intensive products. It has also now purchased Burt's Bees to expand its green market offerings.'

Combining foresight and collaboration at Arup

Market assessment is a starting point for everything in each of Arup's regions.

'We have a foresight and innovation team, and they started engaging with stakeholders around the world, and in the end they ran facilitated sessions with over 10,000 people – looking at what they think the drivers of change in the world are going to be.'

The research gives the business confidence, particularly in terms of a positive response to the sustainable values that it cherishes. It showed that customers were genuinely concerned about climate change, water, energy, as well as bigger-picture issues like urbanization or demographic trends.

Leading companies inspire followers, and Arup has continually redefined standards amongst its peers. 'I think the top end of industry in any country feeds off itself, and generally moves everything upwards as a result of people becoming aware of what others are doing, and that is being translated into what they're thinking of,' says David Singleton. Collaboration is also possible, the industry coming together to agree new approaches, or sharing investments and resources. 'Arup is involved in many cross-industry collaborations – not necessarily with our competitors but in the built-environment space – that are helping to explore and identify new strategies and better solutions.'

Fair-trade innovation, because it matters

'I am constantly inspired by the innovative approaches by the producer groups worldwide. A group of Brazil nut producers in Bolivia are part-owners of the Liberation nut company, the newest 100 per cent fair-trade company. They go into the Amazon rainforest to collect Brazil nuts, carrying loads of up to 70 lbs on their backs to the collection points. The fact that they are for the first time getting a fair price for their nuts gives them an economic incentive to preserve the rainforest.'

The smallholders and plantations as well as the companies in fair trade are constantly looking to green their practices. For example, the sugar mill in Belize processing fair-trade sugar for Tate and Lyle is fired by the waste sugar leaves cut off the cane. Agrocel cotton growers in very dry areas of Western Gujarat in India are experimenting with drip irrigation in order to stretch scare water resources, and are processing their own neem seeds into organic pesticide.

'It is always exciting to hear how each producer group is innovating in how to green their businesses. Coocafe in Costa Rica has reduced by tenfold the amount of water they use for washing their coffee and are firing their ovens to roast the coffee beans with the shells of macadamia nuts.

'And the fair-trade companies are also leading the way. The clothes made by Bishopston Clothing, for example, not only use organic fair trade [materials] but [the clothing is] also handmade at every stage of the long, complex process including the spinning and weaving and dyeing. People Tree likewise are working to bring in new cotton farmers from Bangladesh where their cloth is handwoven, while Gossypium were the first company to work with Indian cotton farmers organic and fair-trade standards.'

6 Engaging consumers

- How to engage conscious consumers through an enlightened dialogue.
- How to use networks, communities and partners to do more.
- How to deliver a total sustainable consumer experience.

Would you believe somebody who eagerly tells you that they are good for you?

Communicating the sustainability of your business practices or products requires a fine line between boldness and benevolence. You do these things because you believe in your purpose, to make a difference to your world. You don't just do them to make a quick buck.

The rush to jump on the green bandwagon was accompanied by a deluge of 'greenwash', companies who were coating intrinsically bad products with a little good: the tobacco company that builds the nearby children's playground, the supermarket that donates books to local schools, the airline that adds an 'offset' button for its frequent flyers.

Sustainable benefits – the positive impact for consumers, and on their environment or society, globally or locally – must be communicated with care. Like any other type of marketing, it is about engaging audiences in issues and ideas that are relevant and compelling to them, and then also considering how they are different from the alternatives (not just the immediate competition). The simplicity of 'green' had its moment but also became a fashion, which can easily revert from cool to uncool, from energizer to essential.

Remember Zipcars, the San Francisco company that hires its funky urban cars by the hour and minute, thereby removing the aspiration and need for car ownership. Whilst it has sustainable benefits, that is not the biggest motivator for consumers – it remains a 'third button'. Instead Zipcars has promoted itself on financial rather than environmental benefits. Yes, it's good for the environment, but it saves you money too. And that is what matters more to its target audience.

Government legislation is increasingly a 'push' rather than 'pull' force in getting business to adopt sustainable practices, based on increased regulation and a few tax breaks. However, consumers are more emotional people. They respond better to the pull than the push. Pull is about listening and understanding your audience, then attracting and engaging them, doing business on their terms, not yours.

Engaging consumers in sustainability starts with a brand that does more for them – it has a relevant and useful purpose. Deeper insights reveal the real priorities of consumers beyond their accepted practices, and value propositions are then used to focus on relevant benefits, introducing solutions that enable consumers to achieve their goals, but in a better way. Pledges and labels can be used to emphasize the promise and the relevant benefits.

'Good' communication is less about advertising and selling, more about engaging with the right communities. Consumers trust each other, more than they would ever trust a business, and in particular the power of web-based audiences can be mind-boggling.

Networked technologies will become increasingly important in this regard. Social networks highlight the influence consumers have on their peers, and as these communities become more specific (people coming together with particular interests or issues), then the recommendation will be much stronger and more important. Affinity groups, brands and associations that support similar causes are likely to be prime early adopters.

Communicating a promise, of course, is one thing. Delivering it is quite another. This is why 'good experiences' become crucial to the attitudes and retention of consumers. It is about bringing together the right products and services, pricing and distribution models, to serve the consumer effectively, and enable them to do more than they could otherwise.

The quiet goodwill created by millions of hours spent by Starbucks employees supporting local communities was undone by the careless instruction to leave water taps running, and thereby save time serving coffee. The gourmet food retailer that went to great lengths in sourcing premium, organic produce forgot to ensure that its bags were biodegradable.

Everything matters in engaging the conscience consumer; taken together, the big and little things can add up to a truly distinctive and rewarding experience.

Engaging people through enlightened dialogue

Ben & Jerry's was one of the first iconic brands to put sustainable issues at the core of its proposition – environmentally friendly, socially concerned ice cream. And, most importantly, it tasted fantastic too.

Whilst the North American mavericks were perhaps more influenced by Sixties hippydom and a backlash against unnatural foods, today's sustainability-minded entrepreneurs are more likely to be influenced by a new world order and the opportunities created through connected, digital technologies.

Sustainable solutions need to be marketed like any other, but in order to be engaging, there are some simple rules:

- Consumers buy benefits, not features, that are relevant and distinctive; these benefits will be partly functional to do the job, partly sustainable to make life better.
- Communication is more effective when it is a pull rather than a push; consumers don't want to be told, they want to learn, they want choice rather than force.

- Consumers want to interact on their terms, when and how they want; speed and convenience matter more than ever.
- Consumers seek solutions to problems, not products and services: working with other partners, linking components and customizing solutions.

However, consumers need help to understand and embrace this complex new world. Therefore companies cam balance their pull with education, influence and pre-selection of the 'better' options for consumers. 'Choice influencing' and 'choice editing' are two common approaches to doing this:

- *'Choice influencing'* is when a business or government encourages consumers to adopt certain behaviours – such as Wal-Mart providing healthy-eating advice to shoppers, or a change in taxation to encourage people to buy lower-emission cars.
- *'Choice editing'* is when a business or government makes choices for consumers – such as M&S removing all non-fair-trade foods from its stores, or Australia removing all non-energy-efficient light bulbs from the market.

Ted Levitt, the great marketing professor, reminds us to focus on benefits rather than features, famously saying, 'People don't want to buy a quarter-inch drill, they want a quarter-inch hole.' Similarly, sustainability needs to focus on the benefits to people rather than features.

However, these benefits need to be relevant to the target audience if they are to engage. For many of the social and environmental issues this is not so easy. Whilst responsible global citizens should not feel there is an instant benefit to helping to resolve fundamental issues – such as poverty, human rights and pollution – it is much more engaging when there is some answer to the 'What's in it for me?' question.

We hear much about climate change, but less about the benefits of resolving the problem if you are a mother of three children living in Paris, France. Obviously, there is a connection – avoiding the dangers of uncertain and extreme weather conditions, how these will change food supplies, the cost of buildings insurance and so on – but it is not a simple message. It therefore requires careful education that, once in place, can be summarized by more compelling narratives, or even simpler images and symbols.

GreenOrder, the sustainable business strategy firm, has created a framework for developing strategies and communications, known as CRED:

- Credibility: why should anyone believe us?
- Relevance: how can we leverage sustainability to create value?

- Effective messaging: how to translate complex data into compelling messages?
- Differentiation: do we have unique goals and achievements?

One of the biggest questions is whether to seek to embrace sustainability holistically or progressively – to make all products sustainable overnight, or to gradually add sustainable products to the portfolio over time. The complexity of the challenge means that the latter approach is the only practical solution – working on one aspect of business at a time, or on one category of products at a time, and waiting until there is sufficient 'critical mass' before starting to promote your credentials and further intentions.

Building networks to do more together

Networks are one of the best ways to reach and engage with people. They recognize that power is now with and between consumers, rather than with companies; likewise trust. Businesses therefore need to find ways to be part of these networks or communities.

People come together with a common purpose and passion. Online and offline, customers are increasingly finding each other in local and global networks. Web 2.0, the more connected applications of the internet, which encourage interaction between people rather than just with locations, and the generation of content by users themselves, is driving this into the mainstream.

These emerging communities based around work or pleasure, essential activities or non-essential interests, are reshaping markets in more connected ways. Facebook and MySpace, Xing and Linked In are examples. No longer do they have physical barriers, and no longer are customers alien to each other, walking down the shopping aisles in mutual ignorance. Now they can start to connect, to act collectively and assert their power.

This will increase as the networks become more focused. At present they are poorly defined in their purpose. People join Facebook to connect with new and existing friends, but struggle to do much else. As sub-communities emerge with common passions, then they will become more active, with more reasons to connect. Fohboh, to take an example in the business world, is a specialist community connecting everybody who works in the catering industry. Unlike the general sites, the topics of debate suddenly become much more specific, collaborative and heated.

The role of companies, and more specifically their brands, in these networks is still unclear. Some brands have tried to form networks based on the common interests of their customers – Huggies bringing together new mothers, Tesco bringing together people who love wine. Meanwhile, other networks have established themselves as brands – such as supporter's clubs and professional associations – and then manufacturers' brands have sought to sponsor them or explicitly promote themselves to the members.

The question is whether an established brand can really attract a network of customers, swirling around it with a common passion not necessarily for the product but for its application: the DIY store bringing people together with a passion for DIY, perhaps. Alternatively, will potential customers form groups themselves, particularly enabled by the social networks? In which case, brands will then have to find a way of adding value to those existing structures if they want to be let in.

The implications are enormous if a brand really can connect with a community of customers rather than just customers as individuals:

- Brands can connect with large groups of relevant customers quickly, through collective and viral-based communications.
- Customers can assert more power than before, shaping the reputation of a brand overnight either positively or negatively.
- Brands can transact directly with larger groups, for example by facilitating the connections within the community, or using its hub as a network distributor.
- Customers can leverage collective negotiation and bargaining power to secure better prices, or to influence how the brand behaves.
- Brands can align themselves to communities and grow quickly, becoming an exclusive supplier, or through co-branding and licensing.
- Customers can collaborate directly, to drive new product developments and secure more relevant and customized solutions.

The 'third place' is a construct created by the sociologist Ray Oldbenburg, in which he describes humans as requiring a third place away from home and work, where a person can interact with others that they have come to know as members of the same community.

A customer community has the potential to be a 'third place', where a group of like-minded individuals who enjoy interacting under a common umbrella can come together. This umbrella might be a brand, and indeed Starbucks has gone so far as to define itself as being 'the third place', or the umbrella might be a broader concept such as an aspect of gardening, a genre of rock music or a sports team.

There are certain essential characteristics of any community, real or virtual. Think of a small village coming together, or a group of people setting up a reading club. The community must:

- primarily serve the interests of the members of the community;
- be sufficiently distinctive and compelling to attract new members;
- have a collective identity – a 'we'ness – but still allow individual expression;
- facilitate communication and interaction between its members;
- create, share and consume value – such as content – between the members;
- allow the members to shape the community's development and its agenda;
- have time to develop its own culture and rules.

Academics Muniz and O'Guinn wrote a seminal article about the application of communities to brands in the *Journal of Consumer Research*. They describe a brand community as 'a specialized, non-geographically bound community, based on a structured set of social relations among admirers of a brand', and say such networks exhibit three traditional markers of community: shared consciousness, rituals and traditions, and a sense of moral responsibility.

Shared consciousness is illustrated by Apple users, who will always vigorously defend and promote the virtues of the Mac with total passion. Rituals and traditions are illustrated by drivers of Morris Minor cars, who flash their headlights at each other.

Another academic, Robert Kozinets, has sought to define the types of participants in such communities, considering the different levels of commitment they have to the community, and how important they see themselves within it. Imagine yourself in a local village, and you can see the different characters emerging, each seeking to participate in different ways. He identifies:

- Devotees: weak affiliation, strong personality;
- Tourists: weak affiliation, weak personality;
- Insiders: strong affiliation, strong personality;
- Minglers: strong affiliation, weak personality.

Any community will have a diverse mix of these types. In the physical world, some people will want to be the activists, on the committees, wearing the badges of office, shaping the agenda. In the online world, they will be writing the blogs, driving the discussion forums, shaping opinion. However, both communities need the quiet masses too, some of whom will care deeply about why they are there, others of whom will be 'cruising for novelty'.

Another way of considering the players in a community is to take Malcolm Gladwell's concept of mavens and connectors, as he describes in *The Tipping Point*. Mavens (experts) aggregate significant amounts of content, knowledge or expertise. Connectors have diverse networks of friends and associates. In order to spread an idea, you need to convince the mavens that it is right, then you need to engage the connectors to spread the idea to as many people as possible. If you can do this effectively, you achieve a 'tipping point'.

In the business world, therefore, we need to understand which communities we should align ourselves to, and who are the most important members within that community both to influence and to incentivize. We need to align our purpose to their purpose, and then dig deep into the collectiveness for real insights. We need to engage them in new ways, and align our experiences to their networks as well as to the individuals within it. And we need to recognize that whilst direct relationships are important, it is the relationships between people and the communities that matter more to them.

The 'good' consumer experience

Customer experiences are most memorable when they are like nothing else, relevant and distinctive, personal and enabling to do things that you might never have imagined.

The designed experience – having eliminated the negative moments, found ways to create a more positive emotional journey, through streamlining and elaborating, and maybe even a touch of theatre – can then be delivered uniquely for each customer.

This is not one person's challenge, or a department's – it is a whole-business challenge. It may even require the cooperation of suppliers, distributors and partners too. It is not just about putting in place the tangible activities, products and processes. It is about attitude and behaviours, service and style. It is about being seamless and consistent, acting as one.

However, experiences are emotional.

To echo the title of the excellent book by Andy Milligan and Shaun Smith, it is about what customers *See, Feel, Think, Do*. They encourage managers to use their intuition, based on all their senses, to make better decisions, and equally to enable customers to be multi-sensory too. We are familiar with the far greater impact of our non-aural senses – what we see, what we feel, what we touch – yet it is easy to dismiss these in the rush to maximize transactions.

Singapore Airlines will leave you with a lasting smile, but they will also sell you a bottle of their air. The fragrance as you board their aircraft is perhaps subtle, but it grows on you and relaxes you as you settle into your flight. Their experience design team spend many hours working to perfect it. Similarly, as you test drive a new Lexus car, you are seduced as much by the scent and softness of the leather as by the acceleration and fuel efficiency of its hybrid engine.

In finalizing the design of your customer experience, consider how you can bring it to life – make it a multi-sensory experience rather than a sterile one. Add to your touchpoint map what you want customers to see, how you want them to feel, what you want them to think as well as what they do at each different interaction.

This might be achieved through a more personalized style of service, being more responsive to each customer, finding ways to connect with them, learning from information in databases more about them and previously expressed preferences, rather than following a standard list of procedures.

The Ritz Carlton taxi driver will alert the hotel doorman and receptionist of the imminent arrival of a new guest, so that they can be waiting and greet the guest by name when they arrive. As soon as a regular customer calls First Direct, the telephone bank, the incoming number will prompt a personal profile to pop up in front of the person answering the call, summarizing the customer's details, preferences and financial background, and enabling a more informed and relevant experience.

The information and experiences of each interaction with each person can be useful in anticipating, improving or personalizing future interactions, be they moments or months later, by the same person or by different people across the organization.

Brands are not names or logos. They are distinctive concepts that become personal experiences.

'Bringing your brand to life' is all about finding ways to make the brand come alive in relevant and personal ways at every interaction. This might be through a recognized visual identity, distinctive language and exclusive features, or service delivered with a trademark attitude and style.

Don't forget the big idea of your brand – enabling people to run faster, to make new friends, to cook better food – and what makes you different from the others who also seek to do this: the most environmental, the most caring, the most refreshing. Then develop ways in which you can symbolize this at points throughout your experience: what are the 'brand gestures' that tangibly and emotionally bring the brand to life?

As you enter Disneyland, brand gestures are all around you: the music playing as you walk through the gates, Mickey Mouse waiting to greet you within the next few steps, the smell of fresh bread as you walk down Main Street, the flash of magic dust as Tinkerbell flutters by, the big ears on top of the water tower, the smile and banter from the street cleaners, the surprise and delight as Pluto waits around the corner, as Cinderella bursts into song, or Winnie the Pooh invites you to try his honey.

Nobel Prize-winning psychologist Daniel Kahneman has found, through research into people's experiences in all works of life, that the quality of an experience is almost entirely determined by two events: how the experience felt at its peak (the best or worst moment), and how it ended. It suggests that the memorable experiences end on a high – spending as much time advising customers after their purchase as you do when helping them to buy; or celebrating when a customer moves into their new home, rather than just selling the house to them.

Make it special, make it magical, make it extraordinary.

Marks & Spencer and Wal-Mart: retail revolutionaries

The differences in size, structure, influence and control between Marks & Spencer and Wal-Mart require their responses to environmental and social challenges to differ in many respects.

M&S – a mid-sized retailer with a single brand and limited geographical presence – seeks to 'edit' consumer choices, removing from its shelves those products (and ingredients) that it considers to be unhealthy or environmentally destructive. Wal-Mart, which offers a huge range of branded products from thousands of suppliers, uses its greater influence over suppliers and consumers to offer smaller, lighter, more ecologically efficient choices to its customers.

However, both retailers have recognized their ability to influence the choices and habits of those who are not directly employed by them, most notably suppliers and customers; and both retailers require environmental and social innovations to deliver sound business results.

M&S's challenge

Clothes-to-food retailer Marks & Spencer has been one of the UK's favourite and most trusted brands for many generations. In the 1990s, M&S lost its traditional focus on quality and failed to innovate in the face of new competitors and production methods. Quality and style were subsequently re-established, especially in M&S's range of high-quality, indulgent foods.

However, M&S recognized that younger consumers – important to the healthy future of the business – also wanted proof of a responsible business approach. They wanted food products not only to taste good and maintain high quality, but also to protect them from excessive levels of fat, salt, sugar and additives. They wanted reassurance that, whatever they bought from M&S, it was responsibly made, without damaging the environment and without exploiting anyone in the supply chain.

M&S was already taking action to improve the environmental and social credentials of its products (for example, by using only free-range eggs in its food) but had not brought these changes to the attention of its customers. Having restored its traditional focus on quality and style at reasonable prices, M&S's new chief executive, Stuart Rose, believed that the time was right to present the company's CSR credentials to its customers.

M&S's response

M&S began with a consumer campaign called 'Look behind the label', informing customers that all of the eggs used in its products were free range, that its coffee was all fair trade, and that it used organic dyes in its clothes. The campaign featured full-page press advertisements, in-store banners, fliers, website messages and e-mails.

Building on the success of 'Look behind the label', Stuart Rose subsequently announced a comprehensive £200-million five-year sustainability plan called 'Plan A', bringing staff, customers and suppliers together to 'combat climate change, reduce waste, safeguard natural resources, trade ethically and build a healthier nation'. Plan A's 100-point eco-plan aims for 'carbon neutrality', as well as eliminating waste to landfill sites and extending sustainable sourcing.

By 2012, M&S aims to reduce energy consumption by 25 per cent, increase the use of renewable energy, double regional food sourcing, cut packaging by 25 per cent, and restrict packaging materials to those that can be recycled or composted. All of the fleeces sold in M&S, and all of the labels on the 60 million garments that are sold each year, are to be made from recycled plastic bottles.

In relation to its food range, M&S:

- removed or reduced harmful hydrogenated fats, unnecessary preservatives and artificial flavours and colours;
- adopted the Food Standards Agency (FSA) 'traffic lights' and guideline daily allowance information on its labelling;
- converted all of its sugar cane, cocoa, tea and coffee to fair trade;
- began helping farmers to generate electricity from wind and anaerobic digestion;
- began charging customers for plastic bags.

Mindful of its broader influence and responsibility throughout the value chain, M&S also launched the Supplier Exchange programme to share best practice with suppliers, stimulate innovation, help them secure funding and encourage them to offer work to disadvantaged people. It also launched a trial of the M&S and Oxfam Clothes Exchange programme, whereby customers who donated M&S clothes to Oxfam received discounts on future purchases from M&S.

Wal-Mart's challenge

Wal-Mart is the world's largest public corporation, with huge direct and indirect impacts on the global economy, environment and society. Since its foundation in 1962, Wal-Mart has focused on selling high-volume, low-cost goods to consumers.

Although its low prices were appreciated by customers, who found the one-stop shop a convenient and economical alternative, Wal-Mart quickly earned the reputation of a Goliath, drawing criticism on a range of topics, including labour rights, the socio-environmental impacts of its products, its political clout, and its ability to out-compete local retailers.

As green concerns began to enter the mainstream, Wal-Mart's initial responses were criticized as inadequate. Wal-Mart was challenged to use its global influence more effectively as a catalyst for change throughout the value chain, from the way it selected, supported and rewarded suppliers to the way in which consumers used its products.

Wal-Mart's response

In response to these pressures, and in recognition of the value that environmental and social responsibility could bring to its reputation, Wal-Mart set itself 'straightforward' objectives in every aspect of its operations. It began to examine its practices 'through the lens of sustainability', declaring an ambition 'to be supplied 100 per cent by renewable energy; to create zero waste; and to sell products that sustain our natural resources and the environment'.

Paramount amongst Wal-Mart's concerns are the effects that environmental degradation may have on its own business, since Wal-Mart regards sustainability as a matter of good business sense. It believes that all three of the above objectives will result either in financial savings (particularly in light of rising energy costs) or increased market share (thanks to more attractive and efficient products) or both.

In 2006, Wal-Mart introduced a 'packaging scorecard' to encourage suppliers to use lighter, less bulky, less environmentally damaging packaging, resulting in lower carbon emissions in manufacture and transport, as well as less waste. Each year, suppliers compete for awards such as Wal-Mart's 'International Supplier of the Year for Sustainable Engagement', which recognizes the quality of sustainability initiatives, innovation and the ability to communicate effectively with Wal-Mart's international supplier development team.

The impact

According to M&S, 'Look behind the label' was the most successful advertising campaign in its history. Brand tracking showed 'unprecedented and sustained benefits'; customers rated M&S as 'the most ethical place to shop', according to TNS Global; Citigroup estimated that the campaign had given M&S a six-month lead over its competitors in the arena of ethics; Friends of the Earth and Greenpeace described M&S as the UK's greenest retailer; Tesco and Wal-Mart – much larger companies, with greater environmental and social impacts – were moved to introduce similar programmes. Thanks to 'Look behind the label' and Plan A, M&S has won many awards, including 'Responsible Retailer of the Year' at the World Retail Awards. By charging customers for plastic bags, M&S reduced their use by 80 per cent.

However, in 2008, M&S's share price plummeted amongst fears that the credit crunch, rising energy prices and dramatic increases in the prices of mineral and edible commodities would hit sales on the British high street. Responsibility for Plan A was handed to Richard Gillies (previously M&S's director of store design and development), whose concern became 'to reconcile the often conflicting agendas of the "eco-bunnies" and the "commercial animals"'.

For Gillies, investments in Plan A are as much about mitigating rises in energy prices and the cost of offsetting as they are about 'doing the right thing' for its own sake. He believes that measures to reduce costs, such as the ban on bottled water in M&S's head office in Paddington, are more likely to be accepted by staff and suppliers if couched in terms of their environmental benefits. He also believes that, by encouraging people to adopt more environmentally responsible behaviour at work, it is possible to influence their behaviour in other walks of life, such as saving energy and cutting waste at home.

Wal-Mart's packaging scorecard has received global attention and encouraged many suppliers to develop lighter, less bulky products. For example, in late 2005, Unilever developed All Small and Mighty, a more concentrated version of its best-selling laundry detergent, saving an estimated 16 million litres of water, 113,500 litres of diesel, 6 million kilos of plastic and 630,000 square metres of cartons per year.

All Small and Mighty was named Wal-Mart's 'Value Producing Item' for that year, and proved to be Unilever's most successful new product of 2006, with sales exceeding $100 million. The success of its packaging scorecard has prompted Wal-Mart to develop a second one for the consumer electronics industry.

The impact of these tools lies beyond simply ensuring internal operational efficiency; suppliers must now compete with each other on sustainability in order to secure the best places on Wal-Mart's shelves, and Wal-Mart's encouragement inspires brand owners around the world to develop more environmentally responsible solutions.

People, planet, profit: the reality of engagement

Nike just does it, sustainably

'Nike is a performance company and sustainability is just another element of performance,' says Hannah Jones. 'But I am very concerned by companies that put forward sustainability as the selling point and are potentially sacrificing performance and aesthetics on behalf of sustainability.'

Nike considers three distinctive groups of consumers: the 'Evergreens' (who will buy organic and go out of their way to ensure their purchase is socially responsible); the 'Nevergreens' (who, as they say, 'will drive Hummers'); and the rest of the world, who think, 'If it's easy and not a compromise, then I'll do it.'

The problem, of course, is that the Evergreens are still relatively niche, and Nike is not niche – it's a mainstream consumer brand used to serving the mainstream consumer. Jones says, 'My challenge is for people to walk into the Nike store and say, "That is a beautiful shoe that's going to help me run, because it is the best in performance, and by the way I know I can feel good that it was made in equitable working conditions too." But I don't ever want people to go into a store and feel they have to sacrifice performance to buy a green.'

The Jordan Air 23 is a great example, because Air Jordan is emblematic of the changes as it has evolved over the last 20 years. Nike wanted to make the latest shoe Considered, but Michael Jordan, who still oversees the range, was concerned about the performance aspect.

'The innovation that went into this shoe was unbelievable. They really challenged themselves. Lebron James needed to be able to wear it in the NBA finals, whilst also making it sustainable. And it was amazing, perhaps the best shoe he's ever done for the Jordan line. When you marry performance with sustainability you get twice the benefit. It redefines premium for the consumer – it now equals performance, aesthetic and sustainability.'

How Unilever is harnessing consumer power

Unilever, as a consumer goods business, is very aware of a fundamental shift in power within markets – from suppliers to consumers. Through the expansion of the internet, consumers gained massive power to influence the future direction of business, and particularly its brands.

'Brands, as opposed to the No Logo argument, are the single most important lever society has to extend their "conversation" with companies, from basic functional aspects to other dimensions of the product, such as where the raw materials come from, the process involved in manufacturing it, etc. If consumers had to choose all products in the same way in which they choose bananas or apples in the small grocery store at the corner of their street – ie by sensing which is best for consumption now – all other aspects of product development would remain invisible. Brands today are the gateway for due integration of social, economic and environmental impacts into consumer conversations. Brands of the future will be those that not only satisfy functional and emotional needs but those that also address consumer desires and aspirations as citizens.'

Arup engages people with 'pull, not push'

Customers are responding well to Arup's sustainable positioning, 'with the exception of a few dinosaur-type customers that maybe we ought to be thinking about shedding', says, David Singleton.

Indeed the design firm doesn't find it a hard sell, more of a pull than a push – a nice place to be in. 'We work with clients to explore opportunities in response to their needs, and along the way you develop new approaches and some of those become part of your solution – whilst others become part of your experience set which you are then able to use on the next project.'

In terms of external communication, Arup's thought-leading research and projects attract much media attention, again a pull rather than a push.

In fact, Arup feels it has been very passive on sustainability, deliberately so. 'When we launched the sustainability policy, we only launched it internally. We put it on our website, but we didn't go out and shout about it. We wanted to wait until we were a lot better equipped, and I guess committed, in our regions to deliver it, which is still work in progress.' Having said that, Singleton feels that if Arup did start to market its brand and offer harder, then it would probably mean that it would have to be even more selective about the projects it does.

Telling human stories about Fairtrade

'Communicating green issues, like all good communications, needs both the push and the pull,' says Harriet Lamb of the Fairtrade Foundation. 'People need to know that there is a problem whether in world trade or with climate change, in order to feel the urgency that they take action. They then of course need simple solutions that are within their reach and are appealing in a positive, upbeat way. So whilst the issues behind Fairtrade are extremely complex – intervening in global trade is not easy – we have sought to keep the message simple and clear: By buying Fairtrade you are helping farmers and their families in developing countries to have enough for today and to build a better future for tomorrow.'

Of course, all the Fairtrade products have to score as highly as ever on all the normal scorecards – the public want the same quality and look as normal. Indeed in the early days, when people still had misconceptions about Fairtrade, they needed reassurance that the quality was if anything better than normal.

Central to communicating the Fairtrade message has been a nationwide grassroots social movement second to none. This word-of-mouth communication has been absolutely critical to telling people about Fairtrade and encouraging them to buy the products. 'We support these local campaigners with materials and information, focusing in particular on the impact Fairtrade has for farmers.' As Merling de Preza, a leader of the Nicaraguan coffee farmers, always says, 'Behind every cup of coffee is a family.'

Being a thought leader

'Companies have to be careful not to move environmental ideas forward faster than their customers are willing take them up. The great green businessman Ray Anderson of Interface Carpet had a hard time launching his innovative idea of a closed-loop carpet business where customers would lease a carpet for three or four years and then the company would take it back and recycle it. It turned out that customers just didn't want rental carpets.'

However, Dan Esty warns that companies have to be careful not to overlearn the lessons of the past. 'Unilever had a hard time in the early 1990s selling compact laundry detergent. Customers saw the small box with the same high price and weren't very pleased. Today, however, Unilever's All Small and Mighty branded range has proven to be a big success. Not only has the marketplace changed, but Unilever's biggest customer, Wal-Mart, has helped sell customers on the value of compact laundry detergents.'

Making a personal statement

In the world of fashion, designers are finding that consumers are much quicker to associate themselves with good and bad ideas than they are to embrace more mundane aspects of life. 'Fashion is a part of our identities – it is how we want the world to interpret us, so affiliation with harmful clothes will not make us feel good about ourselves. As the media report the impacts of fashion, so the consumers will reflect on who they align themselves to, but until we are able to offer an alternative, the consumer will expect the business to take the responsibility as they do not have the choice of satisfying desire elsewhere.

'We have not always been driven by consumption, we can be moved by beauty and awe and it is the responsibility of the fashion designer to find ways in which to offer this sustainably to the consumer that are viable. We look across the fashion disciplines – at design, product development, supply-chain management, fashion systems, communication, promotion, broadcast and journalism in order to effect change.'

Dilys Williams of the London College of Fashion believes that this involves a different type of marketing, a more proactive approach to communication with your consumers. 'It may also include removing the bad option, having the guts to go all out with your new approach. The new offer cannot be a compromise, it needs to offer the same or better level of design aesthetic, fit, style, service and value as the previous offer, but with the added credibility and sustainability that are needed for future business practice.'

Williams also believes that fashion can transform brand and corporate reputations. 'It gives a new identity to a business. Now is the time to show that you have your eyes wide open. Businesses addressing "green" issues are seen as those who know what is going on. This in turn attracts interest from investors and other stakeholders. It can give a new credibility, which in turn raises brand identity, loyalty, differentiation, motivation of staff and ultimately performance.' However, she warns that sustainability 'must not be like technology was in the 80s and must affect every part of business, and its value potential too'.

Building dialogue in a digital world

'Digital media have transformed the ability of brands and companies to engage with their customers. On the other hand digital media have transformed the ability of consumers to block out or edit the brand communications that they receive. The consumer increasingly has power over what they see, when they see it and where they see it. This means brands have to actively engage with consumers as they can no longer rely on pushing out messages and hoping consumers will see them and act on them.'

The big issue for brands, argues Nigel Morris, is to create communication that consumers choose to spend time with. 'This means the consumer has to value the communication. This can be hard value driven by promotion, or softer value around information, entertainment, utility or service,' he believes.

'But engagement is also about conversation and creating a two-way relationship. Consumers are now much more active. They recognize that they have power and they are actively using it. They may want to have a relationship with a brand but they want it on their terms. Also, they have the tools to test out a brand's promise. If a brand engages with a consumer now, it had better be delivering on its proposition. Far too often brands have been seen to promise one thing and do another.'

Nowhere has this been more prevalent than in (so called) green marketing, argues Morris. 'Greenwashing has become almost endemic, with brands and their agencies jumping on a bandwagon only to be pulled off by savvy, informed consumers. Again, through the use of search engines and social media, consumers can verify claims, check authenticity and "speak" to thousands of other customers about their own experiences. All this happens in a rapid and uncontrollable way. Marketing in a green world will be held accountable not just for its effectiveness but for its veracity. That will be a major challenge for many businesses.'

Part 3

Releasing business

'Wherever you see a successful business, someone made a courageous decision,' said Peter Drucker.

My world: Biki, the Barcelona mother

Biki is 40 years old. She lives in Barcelona with her husband and two young boys.

Biki recycles ('There is a good system of recycling and a recycling centre down the road that we use to recycle practically everything'), uses air conditioning and heating sparingly, chooses fuel-efficient appliances, uses water and electricity carefully and educates her children about the environment.

Organic food is not widely available in Spain, though there are plenty of markets with local produce.

For Biki convenience and price are the most common trade-offs. 'I am not too price sensitive if I know that the quality of the product is good and it is doing good. My major source of frustration is in the area of transport, where I drive for convenience, which annoys me, but I do not change my ways as the time cost and hassle cost are just too extreme.'

She acknowledges that she could do more in her daily life to reduce her carbon footprint but feels that these efforts are not going to really make a difference.

'What really would make a difference is when carbon-neutral vehicles are the norm. This requires incentives for manufacturers, governments and consumers to invest in a new form of personal transport… ie tax petrol cars so highly that it becomes too expensive to drive, provide large incentives for the best possible alternative that is currently in the market.'

At the moment she is not prepared to give up the car, and although she has reduced the number of flights her family takes, they have not ruled out flying altogether. 'I see my behaviour changing if my attitude changes (get scared into it) or it becomes too expensive to do.'

My world: Stuart, the London advertising exec

Stuart is 55 and runs an ethical advertising agency in London.

Green issues are always on Stuart's mind from taking a shower in the morning, not using chemicals, to tending an organic garden. He also supports various charities: FoE, Greenpeace, the Soil Association, Garden Organic, Woodland Trust.

He does have a car but says, 'I have owned the same car for 20 years. It is a 1971 sports car and is ethical in the sense that I keep it going rather than buy new ones. Well, that's my excuse...'

The social and environmental issues that really matter to him?

'Vegetarianism as a solution for world hunger. Justice for the people of Palestine and Israel. The peace tax campaign as a way to support peace, not war. Solar energy developments that will see poor countries become rich. Conservation of water and wildlife resources and a proper stewardship of the sea. New economics where the ecology of the planet matters.'

Does he feel he can make a difference?

'Yes. I don't believe the end is nigh! Some of these things anyone can do – it doesn't take much to become a vegetarian. And as Gandhi said, "To believe in something and not live it is dishonest." So I can make a difference to anything I feel strongly about just by living as if I can.'

On the subject of trade-offs, Stuart says: 'Everything is a trade-off, nothing is perfect. All you can do is try to do the best you can, where the best is defined by the least harm and the most good.'

Stuart sees the role of government as fundamental – 'They should be the great enablers' – and the role of business as 'opportunistic but useful – and sometimes more inspired than government'.

My world: Nicky, the Hong Kong banker

Nicky is 36. She is an ex-pat living in Hong Kong, where she works for a global bank. She is married with a one-year-old daughter.

'I feel very strongly that we should look after our planet better because it really is the only home we have; and now, having a child, I feel it is my responsibility … Living in Hong Kong puts a real shadow on this. The sky is grey most days, the air is quite toxic and I know that it will have an effect on us in the long term. There are concern groups that one can become involved with but I'm not sure how effective they are … apathy stops me from signing up … no, apathy is part of it, but so is the fact that the odds seem to be so in favour of the polluters.'

On trade-offs, she says: 'I would like to buy more seasonal, local produce, but it's hard to come by … some local produce is available but it's very limited … Australian organic seasonal produce is on offer here but it's flown in and the air miles don't do anything for the environment … we have one organic supermarket that is wildly overpriced.

'My daughter's disposable nappies bother me but I'm not sure what one does about that as I can't see us changing to terry cloth and pins … I try and appease my conscience by making sure we do as much other green stuff as possible – we shower rather than bath, turn the lights off, recycle, etc.

'Air travel is a dilemma; you have to leave HK to go on holiday, as there are no local options available, and can only fly. We live far from family, so travel is a necessity in that respect. Nothing would change this behaviour – it is a by-product of where we live.'

On business, Nicky feels that 'Corporates are the drivers of the world economy and so can make any change they want, anywhere, any time. By insisting on sustainable policies, masses of good work can be done. The only problem is getting them to understand they can do this and still make as much money as they are now. Grameen Bank is a great example of how you can change the lives of millions and generate billions of dollars with a $27 investment.'

7 Sustainable operations

- How to improve the sustainable performance of your supply chain.
- How to work with sourcing, production and distribution partners in new ways.
- How to innovate operational processes for efficiency and reduced impact.

Good growth starts by being good, rather than doing good.

Being good starts in the depth of the business operations – how raw materials are sourced, how efficiently the products are made, what happens to waste, how the goods are packaged and distributed, reusing and recycling, where the money comes from for investment, buildings and transportation, how employees are managed and rewarded – and much more.

Exploited workers, local pollution, unregulated suppliers, toxic materials, poor conditions, carbon emissions, inefficient processes: these are the things we must eliminate. We need to reduce energy, use renewable materials, minimize waste and technological obsolescence, avoid artificial ingredients and unnecessary transportation, and support the environment and do more for society.

Compliance with environmental standards is crucial. However, business operations are increasingly transparent to employees, consumers and the outside world. The efficiency of operations is under the microscope. Activists are forensic in their search for transgressions as ways of highlighting issues and mobilizing public opinion. Whilst there are clear standards and legal requirements in some areas – such as LEED standards for sustainable buildings – other aspects require your own definition and will evolve over time.

Consider the issue of ethical sourcing in the clothing sector. Every brand is desperate to avoid the shame of 'sweatshops'; and in the technology world, the problem of what to do with the billions of old televisions, phones and computers when they are replaced by higher performance models. Disposal becomes as important as creation.

Working better together

Partnering is an important feature of this new sustainable world – supporting and demanding sustainable practices from suppliers and distributors, or even working with competitors to crack fundamental industry-wide challenges. Collaboration might be in the form of sharing transportation with competitors, or getting staff to share cars to come to work, working with new types of suppliers or others who can use the by-products of your own business. Auditing and monitoring, new standards and self-regulation become ever more important.

Operational capabilities can also be used to go beyond the normal business activities – employees supporting special causes, facilities used by local communities, processes applied to address specific issues. P&G uses its enormous research, development and production capabilities to produce millions of sachets of water-purification powder. Shell utilizes its expert skills in

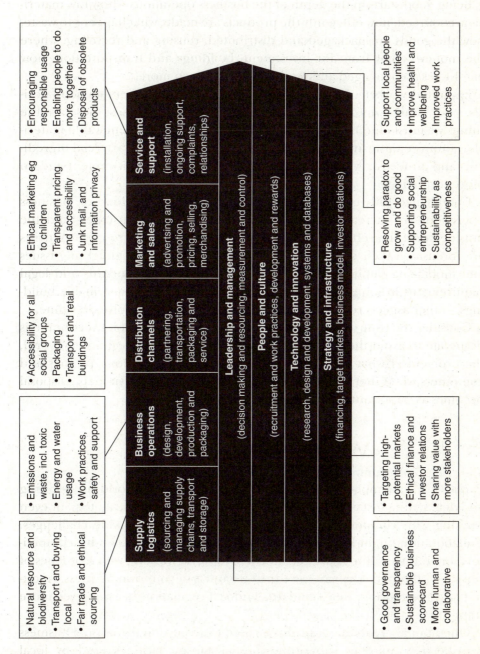

Figure 7.1 Sustainable operations: examples of better practices across every aspect of the value chain

engineering and scenario planning to help solve social issues such as public transport. Nike seeks to embrace social entrepreneurship ventures in its supply chain, thereby creating better products whilst also supporting small businesses and society at the same time.

Some aspects of business are not simple to address. Cars and planes are some of the biggest polluters, and so the search for 'clean' energy sources is more important here than anywhere. Richard Branson, with his airlines and trains, has pledged the entire future profits of the businesses to investment in doing good, plus a $100 million incentive for the first clean fuel to support a transatlantic flight. Warren Buffett has pledged a similar 'X Prize' through Progressive, his car insurance business, to whoever can develop a commercially realistic hydrogen-powered car.

Good sourcing, transporting and producing

Sustainability is still an evolving and imprecise science. Many of the terms being used – such as organic, natural, safe, fair trade, non-toxic, environmentally friendly – have no legal or standard definitions. They are open to abuse, as well as being difficult to live up to.

The lack of holistic standards means that there are few absolutes – few companies who do everything well, and an ever rising bar to reach. There are, however, many standards for aspects of sustainability. LEED (Leadership in Energy and Environmental Design) is a voluntary standard for sustainable buildings that is increasingly adopted worldwide, GRI (Global Reporting Initiative) offers a recommended standard for social and environmental reporting, and ISO 14001 defines the way a company organizes itself to control its environmental impacts.

Whilst sustainability measures are useful tools to help organizations to improve, to benchmark themselves against others, and to balance their focus on the many different aspects of sustainability, they should not be seen as an end in themselves. Sustainability creates a better business, one more likely to achieve its purpose, where sustained good financial performance is the best measure of success, although not necessarily the goal.

The gleaming corporate reputations that have been tarnished because of some form of questionable practice in the supply, production or delivery of products and services are too numerous to mention. But some stick in the memory for years: Nike and its sweatshop problems in Asia, IKEA where some wood was found to be from endangered rainforests, Shell with its environmental challenges in Nigeria, Coca-Cola with its heavy-handed approach to small retailers in India, Starbucks with its constantly running water behind the counters.

Today these companies are notable for their sustainability leadership. Typically when such challenges emerge, a company responds more effectively than its complacent peers – although being a leader also means that you are under even more scrutiny, and any slip can become a big deal, as Starbucks found out.

Consumers demand more and more information about a product and the business – where it comes from, how it is made, what the business does with waste, how much energy and how many miles are consumed in making the product – the list goes on. They feel they have a right to know, and it starts to influence their perceptions of brands and their purchase intentions.

Tesco, for example, has suppliers from all over the world scrambling to comply with its sustainability standards, and scrutinized to ensure that they do. The retailer demands more from its suppliers – even the biggest players such as Kellogg's or Nestlé – from organic versions of products to recyclable packaging, local sourcing and detailed reporting.

Similarly Wal-Mart says, 'We have a goal to be supplied by 100 per cent renewable energy, to create zero waste, and to sell products that sustain our resources and environment.' It is making the change in every aspect of its operations – from LED (light-emitting diode) lighting replacing fluorescent strip lights in its stores, to hydrogen fuel cells for its forklift trucks.

Creating a more sustainable supply chain is partly about efficiency and compliance but increasingly results from the demands of consumers. Environmental certification is increasingly demanded from suppliers as a condition of contracts, whilst suppliers and manufacturers, brands and retailers can also work together to create more sustainable solutions.

A brand that reduces packaging is inevitably concerned that it will lose visual presence on the supermarket shelf. A supplier that uses natural ingredients might be at a cost disadvantage compared to others. A manufacturer who produces only fair-trade goods may offer a more limited range than others. The retailer should work in partnership with these other parties to find ways of accommodating, supporting and making the most of these positive features – for example, by giving sustainable products a more attractive space, additional in-store promotion, or even using a different business model.

Timberland, for example, redesigned its shoe boxes to eliminate 15 per cent of the material used in them, a dramatic saving when you sell more than 25 million pairs of shoes every year. Not only this but a range of its shoes is now made entirely from recycled materials. The company is using these improvements as commitments to creating a better natural world, the world its outdoors-loving consumers most care about. And you can even pick up a copy of *An Inconvenient Truth* in store whilst buying the shoes.

Supply chains also need to be thought of as systems, rather than a sequence of processes.

A 'closed-loop' system is where the waste of one activity is used as the ingredients of another. Nature is full of closed loops – from trees and plants to entire food chains and eco-systems. Business can start to close its loop by recycling and reusing resources for the same purpose, or in different activities – recycling paper and using it for packaging, reusing cooking oil for vehicles, stripping out valuable gases and using them elsewhere. Companies reduce their carbon footprint, improve productivity and often reduce costs too.

The story of a product is not from cradle to grave, but from cradle to cradle.

Energy is perhaps the largest area of focus across the supply chain. With oil prices volatile, companies from manufacturers to airlines have been thrown in a spin by prices as low as $50 per barrel but then soaring towards $150 within weeks. The uncertainty simply illustrates the increasing risk involved in a dependence on non-sustainable sources. Oil will eventually run out, or become intolerably expensive, and therefore, rather than just ride the waves, it's time to start investing in other, more sustainable and more reliable, sources of energy.

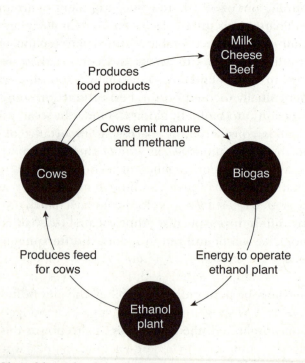

Figure 7.2 Closed-loop business: systemic business models are more sustainable, finding wasy to reuse their outputs as inputs

The power of sustainable energy and technologies

In 2004, Shell's GameChanger team embarked on a journey to identify technology pathways to the future. It used the company's scenario-planning techniques to work with experts across nations and sectors to understand which technologies are likely to succeed and what their impact will be. It recognized that many new technologies do not succeed, rejected by society for one reason or another, whilst others can fundamentally change our world.

Whilst Shell and its competitors bask in the riches of oil today, they know that they are living on borrowed time. Not so much because oil is running out, more because they know that our environment cannot sustain the ways that it is currently being used.

Dave McCormick, co-author of the team's recent book, *Technology Futures*, said, 'The global demand for energy continues to grow, the supply of "easy oil" will struggle to keep up with this accelerating demand and the growing use of coal will increase greenhouse gas emissions. The problem is not that the world is running out of oil (there is the equivalent of around 20 trillion barrels of oil and natural gas still in place – enough for 400 years of consumption). But not all of this is recoverable with existing technology. The challenge will be finding new ways to access and convert these resources into affordable energy in socially and environmentally responsible ways.'

GameChanger initially focused on the new production sources of energy – biomass conversion into biofuels, alongside nuclear, solar, wind and wave technologies. It then considered the increasing importance of electricity in the future, and the implications for its storage and superconductivity. As a result it then explored the convergence of technologies that could have a profound effect on business, lifestyles and the energy system itself.

Ten Technologies to Save the Planet explores similar challenges to Shell, but taking a slightly different perspective. Author Chris Goodall considers how these 10 technologies will be utilized to reduce our dependence on oil and gas. He focuses on:

1. Wind: harnessing the power of wind turbines, the new beauty of our landscapes;
2. Solar: hot and unlimited, the sun enables us to power the world many times over;
3. Oceans: tapping tides, waves and currents – or perhaps we should call it lunar energy;

4. Combined: most power generation emits significant waste heats captured by fuel cells;
5. Super-efficient homes: doing more with windows and walls, heating and cooling;
6. Electric cars: the inevitable switch to battery propulsion, with hybrids on the way;
7. Motor fuels from cellulose: second-generation biofuels that don't reduce food provision;
8. Capturing carbon: clean coal, algae as a carbon absorber, and 'scrubbing' the air;
9. Biochar: charcoal made from biomass that effectively captures and stores carbon;
10. Soil and forests: improving the planet's carbon sinks and regenerating natural cycles.

The opportunity of biofuels has moved on, with many of the plant-based cellulose techniques being rejected because they may use up too much of the world's potential food supply. Instead, algae has become the great hope; huge farms of ground- or sea-based algae are being developed, and whilst conversion costs are still high, it has the potential to generate 30–40 times more biofuel than cellulose, and is not limited in its supply.

When Richard Branson talks about his dramatic innovations in space travel, and the development of Virgin Galactic, he is quick to reassure people that this will be a carbon-neutral, or maybe even carbon-negative, venture – largely thanks to his current investments in algae.

Adidas and Nike: no finish line

Adidas and Nike are close competitors, with comparable product lines, social challenges and environmental impacts.

For both, a key challenge is to improve human wellbeing in supplier factories, most of which are in developing countries with poor records on working conditions and the employment of child labour.

Both companies are members of the Fair Labor Association (FLA), which gathers information on a range of criteria in these factories and publishes the results in an annual survey. However, verifying conditions has proved challenging, because only a small fraction of the facilities – 147 of the 5,187 factories listed in 2006 – are visited in person, the remainder providing only survey-based information. Furthermore, because many of these factories are small and nimble, the threat of an audit or requirements to improve working conditions can prompt them to shut down or shift production to another facility, thereby depriving local communities of much-needed employment or perpetuating existing abuses and exposing FLA members to reputational risks.

With regard to their own operations, however, Nike and Adidas have both developed sustainable product lines. For both, the challenge remains to embed sustainable business practices and innovation in all of their product lines and operations.

Adidas's challenge

Germany-based Adidas Group is the second-largest sportswear company in the world, with revenues of over €10 billion per year. As well as Adidas Ltd., Adidas Group also owns Reebok, Taylormade and Rockport. Listed as one of Corporate Knights' 100 Most Sustainable Companies, Adidas Group has an advanced corporate responsibility programme. However, its 2006 acquisition of Reebok delayed the creation and implementation of a unified sustainability approach. Back on track with a new CSR report for 2007, Adidas has 'baselined' its environmental impacts and made serious commitments to improve the environmental performance of its manufacturing facilities.

The challenge for Adidas will be to differentiate its brand and value proposition from that of its principal competitor, Nike, which is gaining an industry-leading reputation for sustainable innovation. Like Nike, its principal concern is to guarantee good working conditions in its suppliers' factories, where 95 per cent of its products are made and over which it has limited control. Adidas also needs to reduce its environmental impacts, principal amongst which are: greenhouse gas emissions (in the form of carbon dioxide) from powering and heating manufacturing sites, and from freight transportation; the emission of volatile organic compounds from manufacturing; water withdrawals; and waste from manufacturing, packaging and consumers.

Adidas's response

Adidas monitors labour and environmental standards in its suppliers' factories through the FLA and publishes a list of its supplier facilities on its corporate website. To better tailor training programmes on environmental issues, which differ from site to site, Adidas (in association with the FLA) conducted specific needs assessments amongst its suppliers, depending on product complexity and production processes. Because energy consumption was a concern to most of these suppliers, Adidas began conducting supplier energy efficiency workshops in its main sourcing countries. Customized training materials and technical recommendations were developed across the different product divisions.

In response to increasing consumer awareness of the importance of sustainability, the Adidas Group launched the Adidas Grün ('Green') range of footwear and apparel for men and women. Adidas Grün minimizes its environmental impact by being as efficient as possible with the use of the natural resources involved in its production and packaging. It was developed by a cross-functional team comprising staff from across the Adidas Group, external suppliers of materials, and manufacturing partners. Together they researched and selected environmentally acceptable materials that would meet both quality standards and consumer expectations. The final product lines use recycled fabrics and natural materials from certified sources, such as organic cotton and hemp (for uppers and other fabrics), rubber and rice-husk outsoles, chromium-free stripes, and recycled PET bottles (for uppers). Some styles in the Grün range are fully biodegradable.

For the 2008 launch of Grün, Adidas teamed up with the Guerrilla Gardening movement, a group of non-violent activists who grow plants and flowers on abandoned or publicly owned land.

Nike's challenge

Nike is a major sportswear and equipment supplier based in Portland, Oregon. It is the world's leading manufacturer and supplier of athletic shoes and apparel, with annual revenues of more than $16 billion. As of 2008, Nike employed over 30,000 people worldwide, as well as around 650,000 contract workers, mainly in its suppliers' factories in Asia and Central and South America. Nike markets its products under its own brand name, as well as Nike Golf, Nike Pro, Nike+, Air Jordan, Nike Skateboarding, Team Starter, and subsidiaries including Cole Haan, Hurley International, Umbro and Converse. In addition to its manufacturing operations, Nike owns the Nike-town retail chain.

Ever since its founder, Phil Knight, used a waffle iron to create a new rubber sole for his own use on the running track, Nike has made product innovation a core focus. However, in the mid 1990s, Nike came in for heavy criticism because of exploitative manufacturing practices in many of its suppliers' factories. Many consumers, increasingly concerned about ethical issues, boycotted its products, and great damage was done to its reputation. Nike's challenge, therefore, was to restore that reputation whilst continuing to grow its sales, maintain quality and address its main environmental impacts, which are similar to those of Adidas.

Nike's response

Nike, like Adidas, is a member of the FLA, and publishes a list of its suppliers on the web. As an additional measure, Nike began to innovate for more sustainable product lines, beginning with the Nike Considered Boot, hand-crafted from renewable hemp sourced within 200 miles of its production facility. It went on to produce: the Air Zoom Affinity, a lightweight perform-ance woman's trainer that minimized the use of adhesives; the Nike Trash Talk basketball shoe made from factory offcuts and scrap-ground foam; and the Air Jordan XX3, which uses an interlocking system instead of chemical adhesives.

Nike has also outlined targets and objectives to embed corporate responsi-bility at the heart of its business operations and strategy, setting Nike Consid-ered baseline standards as a minimum for all of its product lines by 2011. However, the focus remains on innovation: 'Too often, "green" means less of a consumer experience,' according to Hannah Jones, Nike's head of corpo-rate responsibility. 'If you sacrifice performance or style, you're doing a disservice to the consumer and to the sustainability movement.'

The impact

Nike was the first sports manufacturer to publish details of its factory base, prompting others to follow suit and thereby improving transparency across the whole industry. Nike also claims that its focus on innovation and systems thinking has resulted in sustainable initiatives beyond products, including better demand forecasting and 'climate neutrality' (by means of carbon offsetting) for its retail stores and business travel.

Adidas has high hopes for the success of Grün, but it remains to be seen how its sustainability principles will manifest themselves across its other lines, and throughout the wider organization.

People, planet, profit: the reality of operations

Marks & Spencer's Plan A 'because there is no Plan B'

The M&S approach is brought together and actively promoted as its Plan A. It covers the five key areas of climate, waste, raw materials, trading activities through fair partnering, and health, and is championed across the business by Richard Gillies. 'Health is a key issue, as a major food retailer. Five years ago we were an indulgence-food business, but now we have a very significant proportion of Eat Well range of foods.

'We describe two types of people; there are eco-bunnies and there are commercial animals. The first lot arrive on fold-up bikes and have a very strong CSR-focused agenda and CSR-centric world, based around NGOs based around the major ethical and social issues that we're facing. The other side has been to business school and run most of the corporate world, and they are running by a standard set of business metrics: profit and loss.

'The challenge is that these groups (and this can be the same person at different times of the day) talk different languages, they tend to reject each other. The eco-bunnies think [the others] have sold out, and the commercial animals think [the eco-bunnies] have gone a bit soft.'

However, sustainability initiatives need a business case just like any other business investment, but even more so in tougher economic conditions, he says.

'When times are good, your ability to do things for what appear to be the right reasons, ie doing the right thing to save the climate, or for broad customer appeal, can be delivered. When the economy starts to get tougher, such general approaches to activity need to be focused much more clearly on financial return and very clear articulations of the commercial advantages you are going to be able to achieve.'

Rather than trying to address every sustainability concern, M&S has focused on ones that can make a tangible difference commercially, for example in terms of building design to offset volatility in future energy costs. It's also an experimental strategy, learning what works and doesn't and moving with technology as it evolves. 'We didn't stick green roofs on all our shops, because it would have cost a fortune, and we know that the technology is not right. But we have wind turbines on a couple of shops, from which we get operational experience, as well as having visible symbols of renewable activity.

'The encouraging thing for me is that we spent a lot time wrestling with the top-line things, which is now becoming business as usual. But that doesn't mean we don't have some very big challenges, especially in areas such as raw materials. We are now working full pelt on recycled cotton from industrial waste. All our garment labels, 60 million a year, will be made of recycled plastic bottles. These things are incremental. But it's the evolution we are working towards.'

Gillies has focused on individual engagement. 'What you're then asking people to do is think about it and do some stuff.' M&S introduced a carrier bag initiative, charging customers for new bags and rewarding them if they bring their own. 'We've reduced our usage by 80 per cent, saved 100 million bags.' M&S is seeing a behaviour change in its customers, more recycling, and more thought into why they choose M&S and its products.

Sustaining Arup's supply chain

Companies shouldn't forget that as well as their own supply chains, they are often part of other companies' supply chains too. Arup has found it is frequently asked more questions in a sustainability context. 'Everyone wants to say that they are sustainable.'

The business has recently looked much harder at how it can manage its suppliers better. 'But that's no small feat in a company with a lot of offices and businesses within the offices, and a very involved business model,' adds David Singleton. Historically a lot of Arup's purchasing of, for example, stationery, was from several suppliers, who were therefore very difficult to manage. Cost savings, as well as getting a handle on their sustainability, have led to a rationalization of suppliers, with, in the case of purchasing, at least 50 per cent coming from one source.

'You have to have it all under one roof, to know who you are dealing with and why, in order to start to drive sustainable practices. Once that's achieved you can start to build it into the tendering and monitoring processes.' These approaches build on Arup's existing approaches – such as a code of ethics around human rights – 'But supply chain is one of those places you might be unknowingly violating a human right, so it's a constant challenge.'

Creating a win–win–win with fair trade

'With the public increasingly expecting issues around sustainability to be the norm, the smart companies are the ones who will be offering it now, ahead of the game, and will get real gains back to their company's image and their brand's public perception.' When, for example, Marks & Spencer switched all their tea and coffee to fair trade, they saw double-digit growth in the first few months as customers flocked in to reward the company for showing leadership in making that level of commitment.

There are also more intangible benefits to brands and businesses, including raising staff morale. In February 2008, Tate & Lyle announced that it was switching its entire retail cane sugar range to fair trade within two years. In the first year alone, this will yield fair-trade premiums of around £2 million to small-scale growers in the Belize Sugar Cane Farmers' Association. This, the biggest move by a UK food manufacturing company, sends a strong message to business that fair trade can become the norm.

Iain Ferguson, Tate & Lyle chief executive, said that the move had been 'incredibly well received by customers', with people calling in to congratulate them. He also noted the immediate positive impact for staff, who felt proud of the positive press the move received. At the time, the company had been struggling to recruit a number of senior posts; as soon as the switch was announced, they saw a significant rise in the number of applications.

Although these are amazing achievements, globally it is still only tiny fractions of global commodities that are traded under fair-trade terms. 'That is why over the coming five years, the Fairtrade Foundation is determined to tip the balance of power in trade, taking the model to scale and so enabling millions more farmers and workers to participate. The pace of growth can only accelerate and there is still all to play for.'

Seven million farmers, workers and their families across 58 developing countries are benefiting from participating in fair trade, which guarantees better prices, decent working conditions, long-term and more direct relations. By requiring companies to pay sustainable prices (which must at least cover the costs of sustainable production) with a premium to invest in building a better future for communities, fair trade addresses the injustices of conventional trade, so enabling disadvantaged producers to improve their position and take more control over their lives.

'We believe that putting fair trade at the heart of business is the ultimate win-win-win. Today seven out of ten members of the public recognize the Fairtrade mark, with awareness rising fast across all sections of the population. Repeated surveys show that the public want fair trade, and would buy more products carrying the mark if they were more available.'

It is also – of course – the right thing to do. In 2008, around 3 billion people worldwide earned less than $2 a day, many of them growing crops exported to the developed world. 'Companies can, through the Fairtrade labelling system, play their part in making such poverty history,' proclaims Harriet Lamb.

She is also very aware of the strength of competing agendas. 'Too often we hear that climate change is the single greatest issue facing humanity today. We disagree. Three big issues face the world: climate change, poverty and war. The causes are all related and so too must the solutions be related. And you have to put people at the centre of any strategies to create change for the environment and, indeed, of course, for communities. So, for example, in the Amazon forest of Bolivia, gatherers of Brazil nuts who are selling their goods as Fairtrade now have an economic interest in preserving, not cutting down, the trees. Those are the solutions we have to find – good for people and the planet. Or again, retailers are seeking to reduce the use of plastic bags by giving customers [shopping bags] made from Fairtrade certified cotton.'

8 Delivering performance

- How to measure your impact through certification and labelling.
- How to link sustainability to business performance measures and rewards.
- How to manage business performance and reputation more holistically.

The measure of business success is economic value creation – owners, investors and leaders are most interested in the potential future profits of the business, and this is reflected in market value, or the acquisition price if a company is sold.

Everything else contributes to this objective. Short-term revenues and profits are indicators of recent performance, as well as providing the cash flows to enable the business to succeed in the future. Measures of customer and employee engagement are indicators of longer-term business health, as are measures showing the impact on society and the environment.

Whilst some thinkers call for new measures of business success, moving away from the pursuit of financial results, we are not likely to change the fundamental structures of capitalism overnight. It is much easier to create a better world within them. Their concern about short-termism, and blinkered pursuit of money at any cost, is more a misunderstanding of how economic value is most effectively created.

Social and environmental issues are becoming the biggest drivers of economic value in business today. And whilst they might still be in the early phases of adoption by core business, they will fundamentally redefine the future. They are likely to have more impact than anything else on future revenue streams, cost structures and business risks.

Of course, there are many accepted approaches to measuring the impact of sustainability initiatives, including the triple bottom line, which adds social and environmental performance addenda to a balance sheet, and performance against voluntary environmental standards such as ISO and GRI.

Carbon dioxide has created a whole field of performance measurement in itself, from carbon emissions to carbon footprints to carbon trading with carbon markets and carbon offsets enabling carbon neutrality. Whilst it would be better to find alternatives to using these natural resources and polluting the atmosphere in the first place, carbon management has gained a language and structure that at least make businesses think and act differently.

Above all of this are the implications of transparency in the new business world. Society expects companies to open themselves up to analysis, good and bad, of what they do well and need to do better. It requires a shift in mindset, but it is far better to report the truth and then act on it than to leave it to outsiders to cast damaging and unfounded claims against you, which then stick in people's minds.

Corporate reputations are incredibly fragile in this new world. In the past, a business or brand image endured for years, supported by careful brand and reputation management, controlled use of media and superficial images. In a world of instant communication and pervasive media where people talk to each other, reputations can be created – or more likely destroyed – overnight.

Emotionally, as members of the public, our judgement of whether a company is good or bad is driven by its sustainable behaviours more than its products or performance. Whilst financial success is celebrated internally, it is increasingly greeted with dismay externally. Whilst innovation is exciting, it is also expected. Are you a good company to work for? Do you have good management? Are you a good neighbour? From investment analysts to local planning officers, these questions are typically answered in our minds by how much good we perceive the company to do for society.

However, reporting social and environmental impacts, positive and negative, is only worthwhile if it leads to appropriate action. In the same way that the total profit of the company is difficult to act on if you don't know how it was created, then aggregated results must be broken down in relevant ways.

Corporate reporting needs to link back to practical actions – use of materials, amount of energy, product features – and ideally also to financial results, to make them more meaningful. Linking them further to individual performance targets, measures and rewards ensures that every person is able to understand how they can contribute to good growth.

Certification, labels and sustainable impacts

There are many different organizations that offer certification in different aspects of sustainability. Whilst certification is essentially a measure of compliance rather than a point of difference, there is value in considering which certification bodies are most important to your business and, indeed, to your consumers and customers.

Some certification organizations are public, others private; some are charitable or not-for-profit whilst others are profit making; some focus on niche activities whilst an increasing number seek to aggregate others.

Rather than just seeking whatever labels your competitors are embracing, more important is to audit your holistic impact across social and environmental issues, and then understand where you have most negative impact, and equally where you could make most positive impact.

Examples of some of the different or most popular certification approaches include:

1. Carbon Trust

Independent organization that works with companies to accelerate their move to a lower-carbon business model by providing expert advice, funding, services and accreditation. The UK-based organization works with partners worldwide to achieve this, and in the UK alone claims to have saved over 20 million tonnes of CO_2 since 2001, equivalent to a cost saving of over £1 billion. Its investment programme focuses on emerging clean-energy technologies and helping mainstream organizations to embrace them.

2. Energy Star

Focuses on energy-efficient products and practices, having been created by the US Environmental Protection Agency, and has been adopted in countries worldwide. It works with energy suppliers and building owners to develop appropriate energy-management strategies, and has become one of the highest-profile certifications. Its Energy Performance Contracts embrace lighting, heating, air conditioning, building controls, water conservation, renewable energies and operational management.

3. Fairtrade

The term fair trade is used to describe the wider movement of organizations that seek to work with marginalized producers and workers in developing countries, empowering them and promoting sustainable practices – finding new customers, and ensuring a fair price.

The term Fairtrade is used to describe the work of the certification and labelling system of Fairtrade Labelling Organisations International (FLO). The FAIRTRADE Mark is the registered trademark of FLO and appears on products to show that Fairtrade standards have been met, including a guaranteed fair price and additional premium for community projects. Fairtrade products now account for around € 2.9 billion sales globally, in particular tea, coffee, bananas, sugar and cotton products.

4. Forest Stewardship Council

From food packaging to bespoke furniture, FSC is another high-profile mark in our homes and offices. It promotes the responsible management of the world's forest, and has now certified over 100 million hectares of woodland in around 90 countries. It evaluates forestry practices on their economic, social and environmental benefits, and by marking the forest products with a tick-tree logo, gives consumers confidence that they are supporting responsible forestry. It also works with FLO to explore how small-scale and community forestry projects might also be able to gain added volume through Fairtrade.

5. LEED

'Leadership in Energy and Environmental Design' is a rating system that measures sustainable buildings and is built on a portfolio of standards that address the full life cycle of a building – from design and construction to operations and maintenance, fit-outs and cleaning, and even demolition. The evaluation criteria are adopted by over 10,000 members of the US Green Business Council; by linking with governments, compliance enables access to tax rebates, allowances and incentives from local authorities.

6. Marine Stewardship Council

MSC is the leading certification programme for sustainable seafood, and works with over 200 fisheries from Sydney to Seattle, Edinburgh to Cape Town. Its standards focus on sustainable fishing practices, focusing on issues such as biodiversity, environmental impact, management and traceability. For packagers, retailers and restaurants it provides assurance of provenance as well as sustainable fishing practices.

7. Rainforest Alliance

The Rainforest Alliance is an international non-profit organization that works with local partners groups to develop and promote sustainable standards in farming, forestry and tourism. These standards protect the environment and foster the well-being of workers, their families and their communities. From large multinational corporations to small, community-based cooperatives, the Rainforest Alliance involves businesses and consumers worldwide in their efforts to bring responsibly produced goods and services to a global market-place. Marks & Spencer, Wal-mart, Kraft and Unilever are a few of the many companies that have chosen to work with the Rainforest Alliance. By purchasing products – including coffee, tea, bananas and chocolate – bearing the Rainforest Alliance Certified™ seal, consumers can support a healthy environment and help to improve the quality of life for local communities. To learn more about the Rainforest Alliance, visit www.rainforest-alliance.org.

8. Green Tick

One of a number of organizations seeking to offer a single-branded approach to all forms of sustainability across the supply chain. The New Zealand-based organization operates worldwide with specific focus on food-based issues such as natural, organic, GE free, fair trade and climate friendly – each with its own green tick. Other initiatives such as the EU Ecolabel are similar in seeking to offer consumers a more consistent approach to labelling across the many different facets of sustainability.

9. ISO, the environment and climate change

ISO (International Organization for Standardization) is a non-governmental organization comprising the national standards institutes of 162 countries. Out of a total of over 18 000 voluntary ISO International Standards and related documents, more than 570 are directly related to environmental subjects, including climate change, and many more can help in reducing environmental impacts.

The best known are the ISO 14000 family of standards for environmental management, which is firmly established as the global benchmark for good practice in this area. ISO 14001, which provides the requirements for environmental management systems (EMS), contributes to any organization's objectives to operate in an environmentally sustainable manner. Up to the end of December 2007, more than 154 000 ISO 14001 certificates of conformity had been issued to private and public sector organizations in 148 countries and economies. ISO itself does not carry out auditing and certification. This is done independently of ISO by some 2,500 certification bodies around the world. ISO does not control their work and the ISO logo will not be found on their certificates.

ISO standards directly related to climate change include ISO 14067, now under development, for measuring the carbon footprint of products. Targeted for publication in 2011, it will complement the already published standards ISO 14064:2006 and ISO 14065.2007, which provide an internationally agreed framework for measuring greenhouse gas (GHG) emissions, verifying claims made about them, and accrediting the bodies that carry out such activities.

10. Global Reporting Initiative

GRI is the most common standard for sustainability reporting, enabling a company to communicate its economic, environmental and social performance in a transparent and comparable way. Organizations are required to develop a framework for planning, prioritizing and measuring their activities and impacts in a way that can sit alongside other business reporting and governance.

Linking sustainability to business results

The old adage that 'What gets measured gets done' is still true; and even more so: 'What gets rewarded gets done.'

Targets, metrics and rewards should not therefore be considered the end point but rather the starting point of a customer business.

The wrong performance indicators, an unreasonable performance target or a badly balanced 'Balanced Scorecard' (measuring people, customer, financial and improvement factors) will drive business in the wrong direction. Strategic decisions will be based on false criteria, investments will not deliver optimal returns, people will become demotivated by their inability to hit targets, and investors will lose confidence .

Get the right measures, however, and you can make the right decisions; people and resources are focused in the best places for high returns, and everyone can share in the rewards.

Market share, for example, is an increasingly meaningless measure. Depending entirely on how you define your boundaries, you could have 100 per cent share of one market and 0.1 per cent share of another. As customer needs change and market profitability varies, markets are not equal. Rarely are companies totally in the same market: P&G and Unilever might be big competitors in some sectors or segments but irrelevant to each other in others.

This gives the big picture and unifying goal, but is less practical in enabling day-to-day decision making. Developing a business scorecard, the right portfolio of metrics, should be based first on the 'value drivers' of the business. These will differ by company, but in simple terms there are:

- *Inputs*, such as operating costs, headcount, and time to market: factors that can managed directly because they relate to decisions and actions.
- *Throughputs*, such as productivity, sales growth, customer retention: factors that are direct consequences of operations and can quickly be influenced.
- *Outputs*, such as profitability, return on investment and share price: factors that are more complex to influence but are clearly driven by the previous ones.

Within most organizations, customer-related metrics are fragmented and unconnected from each other, as well as from their financial impact. Marketing people are obsessed with the customer awareness and engagement achieved through their actions. Sales people are concerned about their reach and their ability to retain the best customers. Operational people are focused on customer satisfaction. Yet there is little point in engaging people in great promises if these are impossible to deliver. There is little value in satisfaction if the customer doesn't come back again.

Customer-related metrics enable us to see the bigger picture of business, and see the collective actions that drive value creation. As a result we can prioritize and focus on the value drivers most important to the business. This enables better investment and decision making, as well as better measurement and management of performance.

Within this system of value creation are the implications of short- and long-term actions and effects in the organization: a sales promotion will give an immediate return; building a new brand will take longer for its impact to be seen; investing in new product developments will take even longer.

Short and long term both matter – which is why a simple comparison of this year's costs and revenues is a rather simplistic way of looking at a business, particularly when most of the value lies in intangibles assets, which typically deliver long-term returns.

'Value' provides the answer – calculating the sum of likely future cash flows, embracing both the short and long term. Value-based decision making therefore becomes crucial to deciding:

- *Strategically*. Which are the right businesses and brands, markets, products and customers to focus on for the longer term? In the business portfolio, which businesses 'create value', and which 'destroy value'?

One business might have strong sales and market share, and even operating profits look good, yet because the cost of capital is greater, every additional sale will destroy value.

- ***Operationally.*** What is the most effective allocation of budgets of people and resources in the short term? Whilst long-term performance matters, the markets might still be immature, and the business needs to generate cash flow in the meantime to survive and to fund the longer-term investments.

Ultimately we must combine the drivers of value to the customer, and the drivers of value to business, the inputs and outputs, the short and long term, the strategy and operational implications, and ensure that the metrics we choose are 'smart' – specific, measurable, actionable and timely.

The value of a business can be calculated internally as the sum of economic profits, discounted for the uncertainty of them being delivered:

- Economic profits are profits less the cost of capital. Investors would expect a minimum level of return on their capital investment, and therefore only count the additional profit beyond this. Customer activities directly affect this through additional revenues either from price premiums or more purchases and lower cost of sales.
- The sum of future economic profits is discounted to reflect the uncertainty in this happening – only contracted revenues are certain, others depend on market demand and broader conditions; and costs may change too. A discount rate reflects this. Sustainability initiatives directly affect this, based on the future confidence in the business, ie its economic sustainability.

The economic value of a business as calculated internally should approximate to the market value of the business, if analysts have a similar view of the future to that held by internal managers and if this is reflected in the demand for shares.

Every one of the 'value drivers' can be positively influenced by sustainability, leading to a more sustained approach to value creation, and a multiplier effect in the value created. The essential drivers are therefore:

- ***Operating profit:*** increasing revenues and/or reducing operating costs, for example through new markets or reduced waste.
- ***Growth:*** targeting high-growth markets and then establishing a distinctive position through which you can grow faster within them.
- ***Asset utilization:*** better use of assets, particularly distinctive ones, and smarter allocation of capital, leading to higher returns on assets.
- ***Risk:*** reducing the perceived risk in the business reduces the cost of capital, which gives cheaper access to equity and debt, enabling new investments.

- *Investor confidence*: working more closely with analysts, educating them on sustainability, building reputation and goodwill, with subsequent impact on share price.

These drivers collectively influence the value of the business and thereby the total amount that then can be distributed between shareholders and other stakeholders. The only sustainable way to deliver more value, without creating imbalance and conflict, is to grow the total value and then increase the amount to each.

Business value has tangible and intangible components. Tangible value is driven by physical assets (ie that could be sold off, such as property, equipment and stock). Intangible value is driven by non-physical assets (ie reflecting the future profit potential of brands, relationships and patents). Edvinsson and Sveiby define three categories of intangible assets: customer capital, human capital and structural capital. New international accounting standards have provided new categories for the reporting of intangible assets and new categories for post-purchase allocation.

Managing business performance and reputation

People, planet and profit, often known as the 'triple bottom line', moves sustainability initiatives from the 'good to do' box at the edge of the business to being a fundamental driver of business performance – influencing choice of markets, competitive advantage, business models and brand reputations. Like innovation and talent, this is now part of the lifeblood of the organization.

Sustainability reporting has evolved rapidly in recent years, initially driven by the image problems in the energy and chemicals sectors during the late 1980s. By the turn of the century, many companies were producing CSR reports, describing how they were addressing social and environmental issues. However, they still lacked any common form, and were largely about image and compliance rather than any significant impact on the business overall.

The Global Reporting Initiative (GRI) has brought a more consistent approach to business sustainability reporting, bringing social and environmental factors together with economic drivers. The GRI guidelines are now used as the basis for most reporting – in corporate and small businesses, public sector and governments – and are supported by standards institutes. They describe the recommended scope and detail of reporting, how to

GOAL	TOPIC	INDICATOR DESCRIPTION	FY11 TARGET	FY15 TARGET	FY20 TARGET
Improve conditions in our contract factories. Our greatest responsibility as a global company is to play a role in bringing about positive systemic change for workers within our own supply chain, and in the industry overall. Bring about systemic change for workers in the footwear, apparel and equipment industries.	Human Resources	Tailored human resources management program in contract factories	Tailored human resources management program implemented in all focus contract factories	–	–
	Freedom of Association	Implement Freedom of Association educational program in contract factories	Freedom of association educational program implemented in all focus contract factories	–	–
Unleash potential through sport.	Worker Empowerment	Survey contract factory workers on empowerment/satisfaction	100 percent of workers in focus factories surveyed		–
	Collaboration	Develop multi-brand collaboration in contract factories	30 percent of supply chain collaborated (shared auditing and capacity building)		–
	Excessive Overtime	Eliminate excessive overtime in contract factories	Zero excessive overtime identified in contract factories		–
We believe in human potential. We believe in the power of sport to change a young person's life. To build a healthy community. To create social change. Create sustainable products and business models.	Considered Design Index: Overall	Overall index score	100 percent of footwear product reaches baseline standards	100 percent of apparel product reaches baseline standards	100 percent of product reaches baseline standards
	Considered Design Index: Waste	Footwear waste	Achieve 17 percent reduction from FY07 baseline (in grams/pair) (equates to 155 grams/pair in 2011)	–	–
		Apparel waste	Target will be announced in FY09	–	–
Design for a better world.		Packaging and point-of-purchase waste	Achieve a 30 percent reduction		
	Considered Design Index: Volatile Organic Compounds	Volatile organic compounds in footwear	Maintain current volatile organic compounds grams/pair amount (represents 95 percent reduction from a 1998 baseline)		
		Volatile organic compounds in equipment	Target to be announced in FY09	–	–
A way to inspire new thinking and deliver tangible results. We follow a Considered design ethos across all Nike footwear, combining premium design and performance innovation with environmental sustainability.	Considered Design Index: Environmentally Preferred Materials	Environmentally preferred materials used in footwear product	Increase use of environmentally preferred materials by 22 percent (from average score of 69 in 2007 to 84 in FY11)	Review and reformulate top 10 materials platforms	–
		Environmentally preferred materials used in apparel product	Target will be announced in FY09		–
		Environmentally preferred materials used in equipment product	Target will be announced in FY10		–
Become climate neutral.	Climate Change	Climate neutral facilities and business travel	Nike brand facilities and business travel climate neutral	Nike, Inc. facilities and business travel are climate neutral	–
Nike is targeting its brand facilities and business travel to be climate neutral by 2011.		Inbound logistics CO_2 emissions footprint	–	–	Deliver 30 percent absolute reduction from 2003 baseline
		Footwear manufacturing CO_2 emissions footprint	Goals to be announced by January FY08		
	Contributions	Nike total contributions (cash, product, in-kind)	Nike invests an additional $315 million dollars into programs worldwide		–
Let Me Play Unleashing potential through sport.	Let Me Play	Social Impact	Nike will set targets and metrics around programs for excluded youth around the world by January FY08	–	–

Figure 8.1 Nike's responsibility report describes the goals and actions being taken in each of its priority areas (source: Nike Corporate Responsibility Report 05–06)

address comparisons and timescales, and how to describe performance metrics and the management actions to deliver them.

Whilst reporting can deliver a greater level of openness and transparency, many organizations are still reluctant to go further. The connection between sustainability and business performance is not easy to make but is becoming increasingly important, as the impacts have an ever more significant positive or negative impact on the value of a business. Value driver analysis will help to link inputs, throughputs and outputs, understanding the likely impacts by statistical analysis of past results.

In a world of fragile reputations, many organizations still underestimate the power of transparency. Leading brands like Nestlé and Shell, Nike and Coke have all found that their reputations can be demolished in seconds and take years to build again. Yet these are the companies, given their wake-up call, that are now leaders in reporting and practice.

Consumers and any interested organizations can discover far more, good and bad, about a company within a couple of clicks of Google than any report could ever disclose.

Those people intent on finding out the most detailed facts about an organization's sustainable behaviours can find it with a few carefully chosen keywords. Yet brand and reputation managers are not thinking like this. They are seeking to manage the positive aspects of their products and services, the image they desire rather than the reality they deliver. New approaches, such as Clownfish's GreenSearch, enable companies to manage these broader aspects of their reputation more effectively.

In considering a company's future prospects, financial analysts increasingly regard sustainability on a par with leadership and innovation. They turn to sustainability reports and also to independent tables such as FTSE 4 Good for help in considering whether to recommend investing in a company or not.

Sustainability has therefore become a fundamental part of corporate affairs, of annual reporting, of investor and media relations, and having a more open dialogue with all stakeholders. The challenge, of course, is to fully embrace sustainability issues within the business, and bring the metrics together, understanding the connections, mitigating the risks and seizing the opportunities.

News Corporation and Time Warner: beyond print

For media companies in particular, the most significant environmental and social impacts arise not from their operations but from their influence over

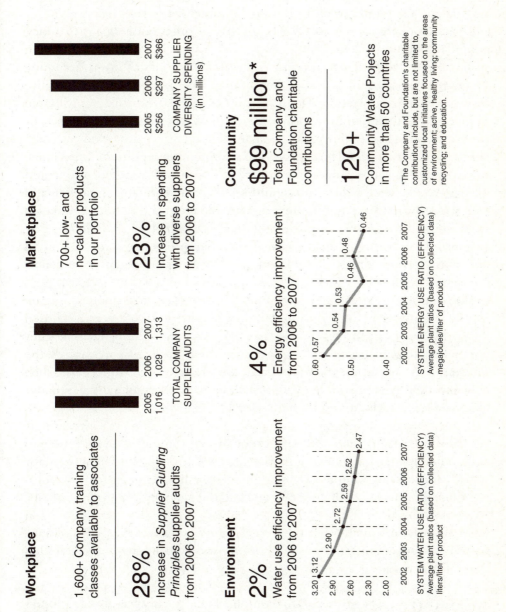

Figure 8.2 Coke's sustainability review focuses on four priority areas and highlights key metrics and trends in each (source: Coca-Cola Sustainability Review 2007–08)

the habits and attitudes of their customers. Two giants of media, Time Warner and News Corporation, have gone beyond internal environmental management and signed their audiences up to a broader effort to go 'carbon neutral'.

Time Warner's challenge

The world's largest media conglomerate, Time Warner, has subsidiaries in all major media, including books, cinema, television and telecommunications.

Time Warner's output has a significant influence on cultural beliefs and attitudes, so its most important contribution to sustainability will come through its content: books, videos and television programmes that educate and equip audiences to adopt more sustainable types and patterns of behaviour, such as Leonardo di Caprio's film on climate change, *The 11th Hour*. In order to do so credibly, and because it is a large company with extensive operations, Time Warner also requires a comprehensive programme to manage its own direct environmental and social impacts, and to encourage its suppliers to do the same.

Time Warner's response

Time Warner uses its extensive data and knowledge of consumer tastes and habits to identify opportunities for social and environmental messages. Some of its initial efforts include:

- Efforts to turn *Fortune* magazine green, whilst maintaining profitability.
- An in-depth feature in *Sports Illustrated* on the oil-drilling debate in the Arctic National Wildlife Refuge.
- Comedy related to climate change at HBO's comedy festival, 'Earth to America'.
- A strategy of 'climate neutrality' for *Syriana*, a Warner Bros./Participant Productions film about the international oil industry, the first such effort by a major studio.

To meet the increasing demand for content, Time Warner has also developed a new Sundance Channel, called Green, which will feature:

- *Change Agents*: a documentary series about the people and projects that are driving environmental sustainability and innovation.
- A series of interstitial segments around the documentaries, showing consumers how to live more sustainable lifestyles.

- Feature-length documentaries and news specials on environmental subjects.

Because it uses huge amounts of paper in its printing operations, Time Warner has also worked with the pulp and paper industries to increase recycling rates, and it participates in certified sustainable forestry programmes.

News Corporation's challenge

News Corporation is one of the world's largest media and entertainment conglomerates. Incorporated in the United States, News Corporation's subsidiaries include 20th Century Fox, BSkyB, Fox, HarperCollins and various newspapers, including the *Sun*, the *News of the World*, *The Times* and *The Sunday Times*. News Corporation's direct impacts, arising mainly from their heavy use of paper for print stock and from the energy requirements of its operations and products, are more than matched by its influence over the beliefs, values and lifestyles of its end users. News Corporation's challenge, therefore, is twofold: to clean up its own operations – particularly with regard to greenhouse gas emissions and waste – and to produce content that encourages consumers to make more 'sustainable' choices about what they buy and how they live.

News Corporation has set itself a target of becoming carbon neutral by 2010. Here we focus on Sky, whose chief executive, James Murdoch, regularly speaks on the topic of sustainability. According to Murdoch, 'It's up to us not only to act responsibly but to help others make a contribution. Even small actions multiplied 8.6 million times can make a big impact.' Sky has spearheaded News Corporation's sustainability initiatives and has set a target to reduce its direct CO_2 emissions by 10 per cent from 2003 levels by 2010.

News Corporation's response

Sky's approach combines efforts to reduce direct carbon emissions (such as using less energy and switching to renewable sources) with carbon offsets. Sky also has a programme of initiatives to engage its employees, business partners and audiences in the issues of energy use and climate change.

Sky provides digital satellite television and other services to a third of all UK households. It was the first media company to claim carbon neutrality, and has focused its recent sustainability efforts in six key areas: 'including everyone'; 'sustaining environment'; 'inspiring learning'; 'building arts'; 'developing people'; and 'doing better'. Sky's environment programme is focused on three areas: operational improvement, supply-chain management and customer engagement. It is supported by an environment policy that forms the basis of its management system, along with a number of defined objectives and targets that direct its activities.

Sky's approach takes it well beyond the established limits of corporate responsibility to include product initiatives addressing access, parental control, learning, human capital management and environmental initiatives. For example, Sky has halved the energy requirements of its set-top boxes and recently built an auto-standby feature into all of its Sky+ and Sky HD boxes. (It has pledged to roll this feature out to all of its set-top boxes in the future.) Sky offsets unavoidable carbon emissions by investing in wind-power and micro-scale hydroelectric schemes in New Zealand and Bulgaria, respectively.

Consistent with its pledge to help consumers cut their own carbon emissions, Sky installers have begun giving free energy-efficient light bulbs to customers, and Sky has launched a website called jointhebiggerpicture.com, with ideas, tips, information and incentives to tackle climate change. In November 2006, Sky launched an online Carbon Calculator to give consumers a guide to their household carbon emissions in as little as two minutes. The calculator provides information to help customers and employees reduce the energy they use and cut their household bills.

Finally, Sky has beefed up its content. In 2007, Sky News appointed its first environmental correspondent and broadcast a week of special reports with practical advice on how viewers can make a difference. Viewers were encouraged to join in by adding local, personal stories to a climate-change map on the Sky News website. Viewers are also shown advertisements that encourage them to put their set-top boxes on standby when not using them; separate press advertisements cover a series of topics including recycling, travel and energy use in the home.

The impact

Whilst Time Warner does not promote itself as a leader in corporate sustainability, it has made significant headway in three areas: paper and printing; recycling; and green building design. Data on its broader efforts to engage consumers in the fight against climate change are hard to come by, but probably represent the company's best hopes for bringing about substantive change.

Meanwhile, at News Corporation, as a result of its industry-leading approach to environmental social issues, Sky leads the European broadcasting sector in Goldman Sachs's SUSTAIN report on the sustainability of corporate performance. Sky has achieved the highest training hours per employee in the sector and high gender diversity of managers. Sky's efforts to address its CO_2

emissions yielded a reduction of 8 per cent in a single year (2006–07), and Sky estimates that its auto-standby facility alone could reduce UK CO_2 emissions by 32,000 tonnes per year. Sky's attempts to go beyond its direct impacts and to influence consumer lifestyles are harder to quantify, but have won praise from campaigners and investors alike.

People, planet, profit: the reality of performance

Nike captures ROI Squared

Nike began to explore how to build scorecards that made sense to managers, linking sustainable actions to operational and performance improvement. Hannah Jones says, 'We began to see people realize that they were agents of change in a business model. Indeed I believe almost every single person within the company has one thing they can do that will make a significant difference if added up with all the other pieces.'

Every manager has their own individual corporate responsibility objectives to achieve as part of their role, with measurements and a scorecard. 'What you do then is devolve power, you give managers the ability to design their own pathway.' She recognizes the reality of business, where just doing the basics is all-consuming. 'People are under such pressure on a daily basis. So the key principles for us are system thinking, ROI Squared, business integration, innovation, and transparency.'

Transparency became an important driver of cultural change. 'It flipped the traditional model of corporations, and we said instead of being defensive about our challenges, how about we be incredibly open about them because people can help us.' Nike began to learn from others, such as Google and Linex, and social networks that collaborate with consumers in completely different ways. It also meant new forms of collaboration in terms of innovation and investment.

Nike is not shy in admitting that it is difficult to measure sustainability in every area of the business. Jones explains: 'We set public targets for the company, and so those targets give you somewhere to work towards. For example, a footwear team knows that by 2011 all of our footwear, all 225 million shoes, will meet our minimum standards for Considered. So then you do the work-back and say, "Right, that's 33 per cent in the first year and 33 per cent in the second year and so on," and our standard goes up all the time.'

At its core, the Nike business is about innovation and design, and so to shift the dialogue from 'You need to do this better for the environment,' to 'Sustainability is a source of innovation that helps you produce products that are better performance goods for athletes,' then creativity flows, and, as Jones describes, 'You unleash hell in a great way.'

Measuring sustainability and ROI is seen as a win-win for Jones and her CFO. 'One of the focus areas on sustainability for our products is how you eliminate waste, so we did a study to audit our current activity. What we realized was that in footwear alone, in one year, we generated conservatively $800 million of waste, for example through materials we have bought and thrown away.'

The conversation with the CFO became a very different one. More about 'There's $800 million dollars being thrown away, how do we stop it?' At the next analyst meeting, the finance director had an interesting new story to tell. 'We are going after waste as ROI Squared,' he said.

Making the impact transparent at Kraft

'We monitor our energy and water use in our factories, and then we publish results,' says Jonathan Horrell. 'On our global website you will see graphs showing the trends of those that are downwards.

'We have now set ourselves targets for the coming years, so we are not just tracking but also targeting our direct initiatives. Many of these things are good for the business, not just for the environment.

'Some initiatives are more dependent on the consumers buying into it. The typical consumer is now concerned about sustainability issues in what they buy, and they now expect to see reassurance. We use data that show the audiences that are most concerned and their actual behaviours.

'Consumers don't want to sacrifice taste or price. They want sustainability elements built in. For example, with Kenco Coffee the consumer has an image that is reinforced with our certification standards; where this comes together it provides you with an opportunity.'

Reporting total performance at Arup

David Singleton believes in reporting the sustainability of business in a holistic way: one report containing financial and environment statements, meeting legal obligations but going much further. The team is currently establishing key performance indicators that will measure and report achievement of the sustainability policy. The indicators are most useful in providing a benchmark for ongoing improvement.

'There's been a lot of talk about reducing impacts, but globally we haven't made any commitments yet. First thing we want to do is to work out where we're at. We're still concluding for the termination of our carbon footprint.

There's been a lot of agitation, including from some of the group board, but certainly from some lower down the firm, pushing us very hard with their targets – we have resisted that – but it would be pointless within a clear understanding of where we are, and want to be.'

Embracing accountability and new investment

'Taking a rigorous approach to sustainability forces you to look at every aspect of your business through a very different lens,' says Nigel Morris of Aegis. 'A key way to get momentum and rigour into the greening process is to be fully accountable. We have been moving to the GRI system and have a long-term strategy to build greater and greater transparency and accuracy in the data we collect. This does take time and can appear onerous at first. However, it is highly motivating for the whole organization to plot progress.'

The Aegis experience is that 'Investors care intensely about sustainability and this seems to be for two main reasons. Firstly because some very active investors that genuinely care about the ethical and environmental behaviour of the companies invest in [us]. However, across the whole investment community there is recognition that companies who are not operating sustainably are going to underperform in future. The cold hard eye of finance is staking a bet on sustainability increasing performance.'

9 Transforming business

- How to define the phases of change in working towards good growth.
- How to make change happen in practical terms with your people.
- How to realize quick wins and long-term benefits.

Change is all around us, yet invisible to us.

Like the metaphorical frog in the pan of slowly heated water, unaware that it is being boiled alive until it is too late, only if we jump to the future can we see the difference, and, like the frog, only then would we jump out immediately. The relative importance of social and environmental issues may still be low, compared to financial success in the short term, but the water is rapidly warming around us.

Transforming a business is never easy, and certainly doesn't happen overnight. It is typically a journey of many small steps, practical not philosophical, profitable not philanthropic.

Small company, big company

Small companies are more adaptive – they can move markets faster, change practices more easily, develop new solutions rapidly. They have a potential advantage in the new business world, to seize the opportunities first, to capture and shape emerging markets, to make a positive name for themselves and put others to shame.

Large companies find it much harder to escape their old worlds. Not only because they have many more dimensions – hundreds of products and as many suppliers; thousands of people and as many processes and practices – but because of cultural inertia too. People are reluctant to let go of their proven success strategies for personal or business gain. People don't like change, letting go of the known and entering the unknown.

Change requires leadership and vision, courage and commitment.

Change starts with a compelling vision, describing in more detail the way you will make the world a better place, and why this will be good for employees, customers and investors – as well as the wider world. You might use words, pictures, video or simulation to bring it to life. This makes the vision more personal and tangible for people, and they understand what's in it for them as well as others.

However, to make change happen, to overcome inevitable inertia and natural fear, people need more. They need to understand why the current world is not enough, why they cannot go on as they are. They need the evidence for why action is essential and urgent. For employees, this needs to be personal and relevant, showing how their business and their jobs will suffer if they don't change. Evidence of a changing world, polar bears on melting ice caps, people starving in Africa, statistics from the IPCC (International Panel on Climate Change) are too abstract, irrelevant. Business needs hard rationales, and emotional engagement too.

Finally people need to know what to do. What are the practical first steps we can take in moving towards this new world? What does it mean in terms of differences in the way we sell, the way we serve customers, and much more? It means breaking the challenges down into phases, into practical actions by individual department, day by day, person by person. But this also requires a plan and coordination, monitoring and management.

Making sustainable change happen

In Japanese, change is more about *kaikaku* (radical reform for a specific purpose), than *kaizen* (continuous improvement because it's good for you). Change is driven 'from the outside in', responsive to changing markets and the changing world.

Andy Grove, chairman of Intel, calls significant market change, such as the arrival of the internet, wireless mobility and social networks 'strategic inflection points', which occur when '10×' forces alter a market with '100×' impact. He recalls how Intel itself almost missed the internet, and in the same way that Microsoft initially poured scorn on Netscape, Intel ignored the rise of Japanese microprocessor manufacturers.

Change agents

He now realizes that reacting to external change is not enough, and argues that organizations will regularly have to make one of three choices:

- not to change;
- to change only when forced to;
- to take charge of your destiny and seek to change before, or differently to, others.

Business leaders therefore need to become change agents – sensing the need to change, then galvanizing, leading and managing the process of change in their organizations as essential to future growth, and before it becomes essential to their survival.

Change is a journey that leaders will need to persuade, cajole, inspire, support and manage their organizations through. It should be driven by market and business strategy, staying true to the compelling purpose and direction of the business, but also recognizing that little else is sacred.

Change will require decisive leadership and rapid action. Everything in the organization should be open to challenge and, if necessary, change. It might require innovation, to start doing new things, but, even more importantly, will be to decide what to stop doing. It will take time and sometimes be painful, hence the need to do it quickly. It must be driven and managed, with clarity of purpose and actions, and continuous dialogue with all stakeholders.

However, the result of change, getting from 'old world' to 'new world', is rarely an end point. The benefits need to be realized, which means the change needs to stick. It would be easy to regress into old ways, or even to remain stuck between the two worlds. Change becomes regular, and maybe even continuous, as in the world of Intel where the market is driven by relentless innovation.

Every business today is essentially customer focused – researching customer needs, articulating the customer benefits, delivering customer service, measuring customer satisfaction. This is nothing special; it is a basic hygiene factor.

However, you can do all of this from your ivory tower, from the inside out, where products still drive the business, where financials drive the decisions, and where managers know better than customers.

'The most emotionally wrenching and terrifying aspect' of any major organizational change is getting people to realize that change is essential, building the extreme intensity that people have to feel if they are to step into the void, step onto the journey. Professor Noel Tichy is author of *Control Your Destiny or Someone Else Will*, the story of GE's transformational journey over recent decades. His most significant insight is that, every time, GE has struggled to wake people up to the need to change.

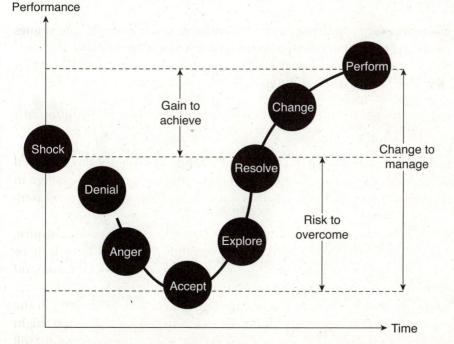

Figure 9.1 Sustainability requires change: moving from fear of change to desire for a better approach to business

Everybody likes the status quo – it is familiar, comfortable, and we find a way to succeed within it. But then change comes along, and pulls the rug from under our feet, threatening our jobs, projects, bonuses and careers. We don't like change.

Articulating the case for change

Making the case is much easier when there is a crisis. But then it's too late.

Change therefore needs leaders and managers. Leaders must inspire people to take the brave step into the unknown, must define an inspiring vision and must guide them on the journey. Managers are needed to coordinate and control what can often be an incredibly complicated process in transitioning a mult-billion-dollar enterprise from one state into another.

'Change' is about transforming the way the business works – both in terms of its 'harder' structures and processes, and its 'softer' attitudes and behaviours. It can be complex and hard work, and could easily go wrong – 'Why fix an organization when it's not broken?' – and particularly so when you need to sustain and grow revenues at the same time as making the change happen.

'Change management' is the process for doing it effectively. Whilst change used to have more of an internal focus, to improve the quality and efficiency of whatever the business does, today change is much more externally driven, typically with factors beyond the organization's control driving the need for change, and a clarity of purpose and priority driving the direction of change.

One simple but effective way to think of making the case for change is in the following formula, demonstrating what is required to overcome people's natural resistance:

> Change will happen if $A \times B \times C > D$
> where
> A = an inspiring vision of what the future organization will be like
> B = the reasons why the current organization cannot continue
> C = the first practical steps to get towards the future organization
> D = people's resistance to change, and preference to stay as they are

The case for change should be made simply and definitively. The vision should be personally engaging, so that people can quickly recognize the benefits to themselves. The reasons why today is not sustainable might be financial or logical: a declining share, rising cost base, new competitors, or how if extrapolated it would severely restrict the business's future. A business case might be helpful, but people step into their known

John Kotter in *Leading Change* has some even more direct tactics for overcoming the resistance of your people to change, including cleaning up the balance sheet to take a significant loss in the next quarter, moving the head office to disrupt old habits and symbolize a new start, telling business units they have 24 months to become number one or two in their market or face closure, and toughening up the performance targets of senior management.

Managing the implementation

Transforming something as complex as a business requires a structured and managed process of change. It can't happen overnight, and is much more than a statement of intent. The change must be driven by business leaders, be managed to mitigate risks, release energy that mobilizes people, make a difference to customers, and deliver results quickly to give confidence and long term to drive a step change in performance. There are four phases to the change process:

Phase 1: Engaging in change. All stakeholders need to understand and hopefully support the change – why it is needed, what it will involve and how it will happen.
  – Evaluate the current business. How effective is it currently and compared to best practices competitively and more broadly? Where are the strengths and weaknesses? What needs to be sustained, changed and eliminated? Benchmarking, strategic alignment and gap analysis will be important in achieving this.
  – Define a compelling vision for the future. This may already exist through the strategy process, but may need articulating in simpler, clearer ways. How does it support the core purpose of the business? What will be different and why will it be better? Employee groups might help to define the 'as is' and 'to be' states in practical ways.
  – Make the case for change. As above, articulate why the current world is not sustainable, and the consequences of no change. Compare this to the benefits of change, the opportunities it would open up, and how it will be good for people too. This process will take time, careful communication, regular dialogue at all levels, and ongoing reinforcement.
  – Engage stakeholders in change. This must start with leaders who need to design it, believe in it and want it. It must be bottom-up, so that it is

**Sustaining
the change**

· Manage the total change
· Establish new metrics
· Reward new behaviours
· Deliver the benefits

**Delivering
the change**

· Develop pathfinder projects
· Create symbols of change
· Take people with you
· Keep the business working

**Preparing
for change**

· Establish governance
· Map out the change
· Secure resources
· Prepare people for change

**Engaging
in change**

· Evaluate current business
· Define a compelling vision
· Make the case for change
· Engage stakeholders

Figure 9.2 Managing sustainable change: four phases in the journey towards a more sustainable business (source: Genius Works)

practical and relevant, and top-down so that it is consistent. Sponsors, shareholders, suppliers, regulators and unions need to be engaged too. It might even be an opportunity to signal your intent to customers.

Phase 2: Preparing for change. This involves mapping out a programme of change horizons – how will we move from to the new world in practical steps, with what actions and resources required when?

– Establish a governance structure. Who will sponsor the change? Ideally this will be the CEO. By mapping out stakeholders, you can shape a steering group to oversee the project, lend support and keep them engaged. Identify a project leader and manager, and recruit a project team with representatives from across the business. Define roles and responsibilities.

– Map out the change. This involves balancing the financial imperatives with what makes more sense logically and for people. Develop horizons of change, so that the change becomes less daunting, more manageable and simply articulated. The 'change plan' should include milestones, timelines and 'quick wins', business results that will build confidence.

– Bring together the resources for change. Acquire the budgets, people and other resources to support the change. You may need specialist external help either technically or to provide a fresh, independent view. Consider the legal implications, including employee rights. This will require business cases and their approval.

- Keep preparing people for change, with ongoing communication. Don't just say there will be an organization restructure with new job roles and reporting lines. Engage them in the wider reasons and opportunities, maybe let them define what the new processes or behaviours should be like, and then discuss the choices and changes required to implement their ideas.

Phase 3: Delivering the change. Making the change happen comes down to people and effective management, sustaining the momentum of change to overcome resistance and barriers.

- Develop pathfinder projects that introduce the change in chosen areas first, then build on this as an example, transferring skills from one area to another and showing people practically what it will be like. Learn from the pilot cases to do it faster and better next time, evolving the change as you go, making it real and simple.
- Create symbols of change. Identify small or significant parts of the programme that reflect the bigger idea. As CEO, decide to give up your large office and move to an open workspace, deliver a new service to customers, consider refreshing the corporate brand at the same time, launch new learning and development programmes so that people know they matter.
- Take people with you. Letting go of the old world and overcoming fears of the new one are not easy. Focus on hearts and minds – making change in culture and process at the same time, so that people have the tools to do what they now believe is right. Keep talking to them, encouraging dialogue, addressing their concerns, sharing your own; be their coach.
- Ensure that the business keeps working. The worst aspect of change can be that the organization grinds to a halt, unsure of its future, and people stop working or at least slow down. This could be the death of the business. Functional managers need to stay focused on today, weaving in new process and behaviours as soon as appropriate.

Phase 4: Making it stick. The change must be seen through to completion, sustaining commitment for it and ensuring that it becomes the new 'business as usual' as quickly as possible.

- Manage the change, with a dedicated change team taken out of business as usual. The programme, built up of many supporting projects, needs active coordination and delivery: actions and resources, budgets and risks. Steering groups need to review progress frequently, making adjustments as required and sustaining the change momentum.
- Develop sustaining mechanisms to reinforce the new ways of working. Introduce a new approach to strategy and decision making, state clearly the new priorities and measures of success. Encourage new habits and

rituals. Tell the story of how the organization moved from old world to new world, and find reasons to celebrate success.

– Reward the new behaviours by restructuring people's key performance indicators, career progression, capability frameworks, benefit packages, incentives and rewards to reflect and encourage the new behaviours. What gets measured gets done, but what drives an individual's bonus will quickly become their new priority.

– Ensure that the change delivers business impact, a step change in business performance, more effective and efficient ways of working, bringing to life a new brand or competitive position, and delivering a better customer experience. Communicate the success, reinforce the messages of the better world, and keep adjusting and improving.

The emerging organization becomes a compelling place to work. It creates a fresh start, to build a new reputation in the outside world, to drive innovation and new levels of service, to change the opinions of analysts and investors, and to shine as a business leader.

Ikea and Interface: good living

Ikea and Interface cater to very different markets – the former to mass-market home owners and small businesses, the latter mainly to commercial property owners. However, both take their environmental responsibilities particularly seriously, and use innovative business models to make them commercially viable.

Ikea's challenge

Ikea is a privately held, international home products retailer that sells flat-pack furniture, accessories, bathrooms and kitchens at retail stores around the world. Its complex structure of companies obscures a remarkable fact: that it is owned by a non-profit charitable trust, set up by Ikea's founder, Ingvar Kampar. The company that Kampar created in 1949 has spearheaded a revolution in interior design, based on combining low production costs with high volumes and high design. In this way, Ikea has 'democratized' good interior design and transformed home environments for mainstream consumers.

Ikea has managed to lower its prices through a combination of clever product innovation (such as modular units), resource efficiency (such as energy-efficient buildings and transport), and innovation (such as modular and flat-pack product designs, self-service warehouses and self-assembly of products). These same attributes help rather than hinder Ikea in its efforts to be sustainable. Resource efficiency and innovation are used to reduce waste, energy use and pollution. Thus Ikea has avoided paying a financial premium for its good environmental stewardship. However, the rapid rate of overall growth – 16 new stores in 2006, rising to 30 new stores in 2008 – has undermined Ikea's environmental objectives.

To make matters worse, most Ikea customers are unaware that they are shopping in an ethical environment. According to Ikea's John Zurcher, 'A part of Swedish culture is to be humble, and that's also part of our culture – not putting ourselves on a pedestal or patting ourselves on the back. But we have also recently realized that many companies are much more transparent and visible about what they do [for the environment and society], and we need to be more visible too. In the United States we have had a lot of discussion about the fact that in an Ikea store you really don't get any communication about what we are doing.' So the challenge for the organization is to find ways of 'commercializing' its environmental and social principles and activities, whilst remaining true to the brand's traditional humility.

Ikea's response

Ikea believes that the answer lies in facilitating behaviour change amongst its employees and customers. It has done this for three reasons: first, because behaviour directly determines environmental and social impacts; second, because habit is very hard to change and very important to outcomes; finally, because new types of behaviour can make people feel differently about themselves, Ikea and the environment. According to this view (which is based on various academic studies and has recently been adopted by the UK government's Sustainable Development Commission and the Department for the Environment, Food and Rural Affairs), behaviour change is a precursor to attitudinal change, rather than vice versa.

To change behaviour amongst its UK staff, Ikea gave all 9,600 of them six low-energy light bulbs, which it promised to replace when they stopped working. It also began a programme to replace all of its corporate cars with hybrids.

For customers, Ikea launched the 'Bag the plastic bag' programme in 2007, aiming to halve the number of bags used from 70 million to 35 million. Customers in the United States and the UK are now charged for basic plastic bags and encouraged to buy reusable Big Blue Bags for 40p each.

Interface's challenge

A leading provider of carpet tiles and flooring (mainly to businesses), Interface was the first company to spot a gap in the market for flexible floor coverings.

Founded in 1973, Interface is now one of the world's leading providers of carpet tiles and flooring. It is also well known for its commitment to sustainability, the result of a dramatic conversion to the cause on the part of its charismatic founder, Ray Anderson, at the age of 60. Anderson was impressed by Paul Hawken's 1994 book, *The Ecology of Commerce*, which established the (now widely applied) concept of industrial ecology. (If you have seen a film called *The Corporation*, you will remember Anderson's moving testimony.) Anderson took it upon himself and the company he founded – a company with considerable environmental impacts – to become ecologically 'restorative'.

Interface's response

Ray Anderson's conversion to the environmental cause prompted *Fast Company* magazine to describe him as 'a radical who makes the folks from Greenpeace look timid. Central to Anderson's new vision was the adoption of a new service model, away from the sale of carpets and towards the provision of carpeting. Anderson applied his knowledge of ecology to the design of this new business model, taking particular account of the mutually dependent nature of different actors and elements in the system. Instead of selling carpets that then became the responsibility of customers to dispose of at the end of their useful lives, Interface leased the carpets, replaced and recycled them, all under a single contract. The modular nature of the product (tiles) means that carpets can be partially replaced, saving waste. Once used, the products are reclaimed and recycled into new carpets or downgraded for secondary use, creating a "waste-free" or "closed-loop" system.'

Key to the organization's success was the development of a comprehensive internal communication platform called Mission Zero, the aim of which is to 'eliminate any negative impact [that Interface] may have on the environment by the year 2020'. In essence, Mission Zero is a communications strategy that allows all of Interface's constituent companies to tell a consistent story about its commitments and approach to sustainability. Mission Zero has facilitated the education, behavioural change and unity of the Interface family; it is the screen through which all decisions, executive or commercial, are filtered.

Since Interface began acting to mitigate climate change in 1996, it has become a recognized leader in corporate sustainability. To pass on its knowledge and experience in this field, Interface set up a consultancy division called Interface RAISE, which has helped many other companies and suppliers to improve their impacts.

The impact

Since 'Bag the plastic bag' began, 92 per cent of Ikea's customers have stopped buying the plastic bags. The scheme has been so successful that Ikea has now phased out plastic bags completely in the United States and the UK.

Ikea's model appears to innately consider sustainability in all possible areas. The product design and development teams encourage anti-obsolescent aesthetics, endeavouring to have its current collection complement previous ones, allowing consumers to buy pieces rather than complete sets. The flat-pack and self-assembly approach, that became an invaluable differentiator for the brand, also lends itself to the principles of sustainability, not only through efficient distribution but also through energy consumption in assembly and all along the supply chain.

Ikea has made commitments to efficiency and green leadership, and evidently will continue to engage its consumers and internal audiences as its sustainability becomes even more ingrained within the brand's products and services. Just as its flat-pack products encourage the consumer to participate in the products, so too should the consumer participate in sustainability, as it is only through active involvement that behaviour change and choice editing can occur.

Interface's new business model, its conversion to leasing, and its foundation of Interface RAISE have brought dividends both for the environment and the bottom line.

As of June 2004, Interface's carpet reclaim programme, ReEntry, has prevented 57 million lbs of carpet from entering landfill, of which 52 per cent has been recycled. The energy use per unit of carpet has been reduced by 45 per cent compared with 1996 levels. There has been a 60 per cent reduction in absolute greenhouse gas emissions since 1996, while 16 per cent of Interface's global energy consumption comes from renewable sources.

Since 1996, Interface has saved over $330 million in cumulative costs due to its QUEST waste-reduction programme. Since that date, reductions in waste – including a 65 per cent reduction in the amount sent to landfill – have saved the company $336 million, according to The Climate Group.

However, challenges still remain, of which the most notable derives from relatively short periods of ownership of commercial properties. Many commercial leases expire before the full benefits of Interface's leasing system can be reaped, resulting in the effective over-capitalization of commercial properties.

People, planet, profit: the reality of transformation

Moving through the gears with Nike

Nike is a world leader in sustainable business practices. However, we need to look at the company's history to understand how it got there. The business, founded by Phil Knight in the early seventies, was one of the first to address issues around employment rights and working conditions, spurred into action by exposure of its imperfections.

Hannah Jones, Nike's global VP for sustainability, says, 'I think we are lucky as in some ways we got a head start on the journey. And I always talk about corporate responsibility as a journey, because I think no one has written the definitive book on it, and because I think all of us are just going through these generations of learning. I'm not sure you can leapfrog the generations of learning.

'John Elkington talks about the different gears of embracing sustainability. Nike was really in first gear, on the defence, and we mishandled it pretty badly. We didn't have these issues on our radar, and it was the first time that activists had really managed to associate a social or environmental issue with a big brand in order to get the public mobilization.'

Nike began to embrace sustainability as a form of risk management. 'But we realized that being defensive wasn't going to get us anywhere, and when we peeled back the onion and began to think about these issues, we realized there was so much complexity. We couldn't change on our own.

'Second gear was about stakeholder engagement – going out [and] meeting with our harshest critics and saying we need to sit down and see if we can find a shared vision here. We may not agree on how we get there in the worst-case scenario, but let's be clear, Nike wants to see equity in the supply chain as much as you.' The business started to embrace a more positive forward-looking perspective, and collaborating in new ways led to a more constructive dialogue with governments, trade unions and activists.

Jones remembers that 'At the time, there was the Johannesburg summit, the Rio summit, and people were beginning to talk about multi-stakeholder partnerships as one of the only ways forward for the millennium development goals, and so our journey is kind of a parallel to this bigger journey.' System change became important.

Then about four years ago, Nike regrouped, recognizing that it would need to be much more transparent, publish more detailed CSR reports on a regular basis. 'When you get together all the data, you sit down and look at them and start to see trends, where things are working and where they are not working.' Nike needed to make the sustainability business case more tangible, and developed a concept called ROI Squared. 'It enables you to show the return to business profitability as well as to the environment and social; it's your blended values.'

In 2005 Nike hit the pause button and said to itself, 'OK, we've been doing this now for a decade, we've advanced hugely on issues around working conditions, environment and community, but is this really how we want to go forward?' The sustainability team sat down with senior management asking what role did they think corporate responsibility should play in the business strategy going forward. It was unequivocal. They said, 'Actually, we think intuitively this is a huge added value for us, could be a source of competitive differentiation, and potentially key to our business and how we go forward.'

Nike believes it has become a much better listening and learning organization. 'Even senior management who had been pretty isolated to their particular world around athletes and sports were very cognizant that there was a very significant shift going on in the world around us.'

Nike's new approach has been based on the principle that sustainability 'needs to stop being a risk management function and become an innovation and growth function for the business'. As Jones herself puts it, 'My mandate is how do I transform a corporate responsibility team into an innovation and R&D team for business modelling for the company. We're searching for a whole new name and don't know what to call ourselves!'

Implementing the 'brand imprint' at Unilever

At Unilever, Santiago Gowland believes transforming business starts by deepening the understanding of business impacts, then committing to reverting our negative impacts either individually, when they can be managed, or engaging the whole industry in changing the rules of the game.

'The first step at Unilever has been to deepen our understanding of the backward and forward linkages of our business operations and the ripple effects we produced in communities and the environment. We had been reporting on our direct impacts for more than a decade but indirect and induced impacts, where our influence could play a major role, were not paid much attention.'

He explains how the Brand Imprint methodology, developed in partnership with Clownfish, has helped Unilever to fully capture its business impact at an operational level. 'That's why we decided to interrogate the full value chain of each of our major categories and brands through this new methodology.

'Brand Imprint applies a systematic approach to auditing value-chain impacts and societal mega-trends that will impact business in the future. The essence of brand imprint is to get an objective picture of given category (eg Tea) and given brand (eg Lipton) impacts. Once that objective picture is obtained by life-cycle and value-chain analysis, using external stakeholders to challenge our thinking, we confront the impacts with societal mega-trends, using our best consumer marketing insights methodologies internally.

'This inside-out and outside-in process allows us to identify areas of priority, issues that need cross-industry engagement to be solved, issues that can fuel brand innovation and product design and become competitive advantages for the brand, and how this links with the overall Unilever corporate strategy. We ran this process in more than 10 brands with turnover in excess of €1 billion and the impact this is having has stretched our thinking as a company and the role we play in society. This thinking is more recently being fed into the next stages of development of our corporate brand.'

Planning with flexibility at M&S

Gillies describes Plan A. 'It's a five-year plan. One year into it and I know that most of it is working, but probably not leading edge as everyone else now has a plan and things do move.' He describes the need for flexibility as sustainability evolves as a discipline and better approaches are developed. 'For example, we've suspended our activities on biofuels at the moment because the agenda has moved.

'At the moment this business is judged against a standard set of financial metrics.' If M&S started to measure against any other criteria, then others would just reinterpret them financially, he suspects. 'They would only squirt our numbers through their old boxes and say, 'Oh, you're not performing.' So we have to make sure that at the moment we are finding the ways of delivering against the standard business metrics.' However, M&S are extending the use of life-cycle costing and scenario planning around future energy and oil prices, raw-materials supply and costs, 'which means that our model can be a little bit more elaborate than before, but we are still working to the existing metrics'.

Getting onto the sustainability agenda

'The hardest challenge of all has been to get fair trade onto companies' agendas in the first place,' says Harriet Lamb at the Fairtrade Foundation. 'Now fair trade is quite in fashion but it was an uphill battle in the early days when we were stuck in a chicken-and-egg situation: we could not prove that customers would buy fair-trade products until companies offered them, and they would not risk offering them until we could prove that the public would buy them.

'However, it remains tough for companies to make the resource investments that fair trade requires. Put simply, it does cost more, because at the heart of the system is a requirement to pay fair prices and to invest in working with farmers for the long term. That's not always easy or cheap in the short term, which can be daunting for companies. However, once they do engage with fair trade, there are of course immediate and long-term benefits – because their customers respond positively, because it enhances their brand image, because their staff morale is lifted by seeing their company "do the right thing".

'It has also been difficult finding the right balance between aiming for high environmental standards – which many consumers expect of fair trade and farmers ultimately want to reach – whilst not setting the bar too high for poor farmers to meet those standards. That remains tough.'

Making it real for people

'The hardest thing for us was convincing the leadership of the firm that we needed to now come up to the mark,' recalls Arup's David Singleton. With the principles accepted, it was hard to get people to want to do more. 'But once you get a commitment from the whole board, it makes implementation much easier,' he adds. 'But we're not out of the woods by any means, as we still sometimes ask ourselves whether we need to do things [that] are obvious given our values and policies.'

Singleton describes his admiration for what some of the big retailers are doing, companies like Tesco and Marks & Spencer. 'I think more than anything else the activities of those organizations are making ordinary people, without wanting to sound patronizing, think about these issues – helping people understand what sustainability really means and what they can do about it.'

10 Emerging futures

- How to interpret the future of business and sustainability.
- How to reconcile good and growth through radical innovation.
- How to learn from the inspirational pioneers of the new business world.

It is a piece of scrubland, about 20 kilometres along the main road from Abu Dhabi.

It doesn't look like much. Indeed it takes some imagination to take in the scale and significance of what is planned to be built on this dry, cracked land.

It will be the world's first and largest eco-city. With 50,000 residents and no cars, it will rise from the desert as a $22-billion high-technology showcase of how we can live, work and play in a better way.

Designed by British architect Lord Foster, Masdar City is expected to be completed by 2016, and as it happens is being funded by the oil-rich Sultan Al Jabar. The 6.5-square-km, environmentally friendly city will be suspended on stilts 5 metres above the ground to increase air circulation and reduce the heat from the desert floor.

It will be split into three decks that separate transport from residential and public spaces. On the lower deck, people will travel in carbon-neutral personal-transport pods, guided by sensors and touch screens. On the second level, you will find homes, shops and businesses, vehicle free except for Segways and cycles. Above, a light rapid railway will transport people between Masdar and other cities.

Water will come from dew and a solar-powered desalination plant requiring 8,000 cubic metres, compared to the more usual 20,000 cubic metres. Dirty water will be used for irrigation. Electricity will be generated by solar panels on every roof whilst also doubling as sunshades, to reduce the need for air conditioning. Organic waste will be converted into fuel for power plants, non-organic waste will be recycled. Overall the city will use about 200 megawatts of energy, about a quarter of that required by other cities of a similar size.

It will produce zero waste and emit zero carbon.

Looking ahead

Good growth is about thinking ahead, anticipating the new markets and opportunities that will grow fastest in the future, and the new products and applications that will be most demanded. It's about creating entirely new business, or at least new business models for existing markets.

What will happen as the scenarios of 2050 get closer? Will environmental meltdown move the agenda from growth to survival, or will business have become the catalyst for new ways of living and working, consuming and prospering?

As the balance of power shifts from West to East, will the West be able to shrink its carbon emissions to the levels of Africa, and the fragile climate cope with the rising industrialization of the East? As the population explodes, and the new middle classes become more demanding, how will people reconcile their desire for more with the need to consume less? Or will technological innovation enable us to do both?

Will all this convert to economic growth?

And will the world be a happier place, where people smile and nature prospers, where business and society work together to improve our lives?

Adapting to change will be one of our biggest challenges, anticipating and responding to a changing world that is invisible to us day by day, but which is rapidly changing the context and future of business.

It demands that we stay on the edge of new ideas, be first to identify new opportunities and seize new possibilities. Just like entrepreneurs and business innovators have always done, but in the context of a fragile and interdependent world. It requires us to stretch beyond our comfort zones, to see the bigger picture, to reprioritize what matters most.

The leaders of this new business world will recognize that being and doing good lie at the heart of their personal and business growth.

Leading in the new business world

Consider yourself a decade from now. How will you live and work? What business will you be in? What difference will you make? Consider one business manager who sat down in 2010 and dreamed about what a day in his working life would be like in 2020.

My name is Joachim Cruz, CEO of BlueSkies, the clean travel company. I was born in Santiago, studied in Beijing and now live in Copenhagen.

Back in 2010 BlueSkies was seen as a small, 'alternative' company, the kind of people who eat muesli and wear sandals but don't understand the disciplines of finance, distribution and management. Back then people laughed, particularly those big old state-funded airlines and traditional retailers.

Now we are the ones in demand, shaping the future of travel, enabling billions of people to explore the world for the first time, without damaging the environment and local communities. And we've sustained profitable growth every year for the last decade too.

This is my typical day in what has become known as the new business world.

0730 The fair-trade coffee smells good as I step out of the solar-powered shower, preparing for a busy morning with the investment analysts. They are about to give their verdict on the 'blue' business strategy that I've been implementing for the last couple of years. My vision is of a travel company that makes a positive contribution to the people and environments wherever we operate, whilst also creating an extraordinary experience for our customers and employees too.

0800 I walk my two young daughters to school and then head off to my local business lounge. It's so much better than sitting in traffic jams, and also means that I see more of my family too. After a quick workout in the gym, I talk to colleagues and prepare my speech. I prefer to use the virtual office and document store provided by Cloud, a wireless worktop that can be accessed anywhere in the world at any time. It was developed by the Estonian innovators at Skype.

0930 I instant-message with a Shenzhen journalist keen to hear what I will be telling the analysts (Shenzhen is the new Wall Street). 'No one back in 2009 forecast what would happen to the price of carbon, or imagined how scarce oil would become,' I try to explain. Investing almost €1 billion in algae farms had puzzled many people at the time. But consumers have responded to this new approach, and we are now able to offer travel with the lowest emissions, and therefore prices, in the world. In fact, we will soon be carbon negative – adsorbing more than we emit.

1000 I jump into my beautiful Tesla from Zipcars, the urban hourly car rental firm. They have a new range of hydrogen-fuelled vehicles that are incredibly easy to drive, with efficient navigation, and they just look incredibly cool too. I don't feel I need to own a car, but sometimes they are still useful. Most of the time I try to support the shared transport schemes that we have set up in the local community.

1100 The analysts' meeting is a very collaborative affair – gone is the macho aggression when everyone was obsessed with the size and speed of financial returns. These analysts are looking at the long term, wanting to ensure that their investments deliver a sustained positive return financially but also have a positive social and environmental impact. This reduces risk, and improves the sustainability quotient – the two drivers of any company's health, credit score and ultimately market value. It goes well, they are impressed by the way BlueSkies has decoupled growth and emissions, and embraced the clean technology agenda.

1300 Vegetarian lunch with a number of supply and distribution partners (BlueSkies doesn't do meat – think of all that methane from the cows). Partners are part of the business ecosystem, sharing strategy and resources. Having them around is also a great source of ideas for efficiency and innovation, and of course they share in the rewards of success.

1400 Teamwork – today I'm working with one of my teams on a collaborative innovation project called 'Blueworld'. It brings together many of our competitors, which they found strange at first, but then realized the benefits in sharing ideas and resources. Rather than all competing for the average consumer (who's that?) we all tend to target different audiences.

1500 Time to collect my girls from school. Happiness is high on every CEO's agenda these days, both for me and my people. Having a balanced work and personal life means a lot. In fact, we offer our employees a really fantastic portfolio of work benefits – from free biopower to time off doing community projects.

1600 Cloud call with the leaders of a social entrepreneurial venture that we are incubating at our research centre in Istanbul. This city is really buzzing as a bridge between Eastern entrepreneurs and Western corporations. The venture is developing a new fabric that we will be using for our interiors, made from recycled car tyres and employing many of the unskilled immigrants from the drought-ridden Middle East.

1700 Time to go to the CPH Travelport and lend a hand with this evening's departures. I see my role as CEO being a people rather than a desk job – the desktop takes care of the paperwork. And nothing matters more than spending time with my colleagues and passengers. Most of our Asian flights depart from Europe in the evening because of the time zones, and therefore it's the busiest time of the day (few people fly to the United States these days).

Out of the window I catch a sight of Virgin Galactic preparing for take-off. It still takes your breath away. Today's astronauts are off on a 24-hour excursion, some carrying out important research, others just for the day trip, living beyond their wildest dreams.

1830 Dinner tonight. My wife and I have invited some friends from Jakarta. I remember people talking about how the biggest change in global population would be the emerging middle class – billions of people who have escaped the poverty trap and are now making their ambitions come to life.

2100 A short Cloud call with our Rio team. Clean travel has really taken off in Brazil, now the world's second most vibrant economy. Here the people from the so-called 'bottom of the pyramid' can now explore the world and share the same education, enjoy as good entertainment, and explore the same places as the wealthiest people on the planet.

2200 I crack open a bottle of my new organic red wine – a funky tempranillo and boysenberry fusion. Superfoods. This is superplonk. The long, warm summers have enabled me to establish a thriving vineyard in my back garden. There have to be some benefits to global warming (although at least the threat has now receded and we are on course for Obama's 2050 baseline). Yes, the world's changed a lot, and thankfully for the better. Time for bed.

Sustainable innovation and lifestyles

James Lovelock was one of the first to raise the alarm bells of climate change. In his new book, *The Vanishing Face of Gaia*, he warns that climate disaster is imminent – we are hurtling towards a hot world where billions will starve and ecosystems will collapse. It is a horror that none of us wants to contemplate, says Lovelock, but it's time we did.

Lovelock brings together the latest alarming observations on the declining number of species, the rate of deforestation, the accelerating decline in Arctic ice and the relentless rise in sea levels. The IPCC previously claimed that the Arctic summer sea ice will have vanished by the end of the 21st century but now says it could happen within 20 years. This all matters, Lovelock explains, because of the 'albedo flip' – ice reflects sunlight, a dark iceless sea absorbs it, and moving from one to the other creates a radical change that could also start to melt the Arctic permafrost and release huge amounts of greenhouse gases held within it.

Just like an ice-cold drink, it stays cool until the ice cubes melt, and then warms rapidly.

While only 2 per cent of the world's land is less than 10 metres above the mid-side sea level, it is inhabited by 10 per cent of the world's population. A 5-metre rise could submerge large parts of cities, including London, New York, Sydney, Mumbai and Tokyo, and leave surrounding areas vulnerable to tidal surges. Shanghai has an average elevation of only 4 metres, and whole regions of Florida, the Netherlands and Bangladesh would vanish too.

Add to all of this evidence the rapidly growing population that destroys its natural habitat and fellow species at a rate not seen since the death of the dinosaurs. Many people say that this shrinking, warming environment will never be able to support the 9 billion people estimated to be living on planet Earth by 2050.

As Albert Einstein once said, we cannot solve this problem with the same thinking that created it. We need to think and act differently.

Innovations will be both radical and incremental. Each one of us, doing our little bit, really can change the world 'one light bulb at a time'. But we need more stimulus than that. The scale is so great, and the challenge so urgent, that we need change of a far greater magnitude.

We need business to rise to the challenge of changing the way we live and work. Business is unmatchable in its power to create change in this way, but it needs the incentive to do so. Growth is that opportunity. The old, narrow-minded industrial world has run out of opportunities for growth. We need new ones. This might be in new technologies, new markets, or by doing what we do in new ways.

Visions of sustainable innovation

These snapshots of the future business give examples of how clean technologies and renewable energies offer much scope for business, either in the development of new markets and products, or by addressing existing markets and products more responsibly and effectively.

1. **Getting back to nature**
    For centuries we paid little attention to the destruction of animals – particularly the less friendly types. Yet we now know that eliminating any animals and plants – whether sharks or snakes, moss or maple trees – can have a devastating impact on food chains and ultimately eco-systems and ourselves. Biodiversity is becoming an even greater challenge than climate change, but one over which we could have more control through responsible management. This doesn't require government controls, it

Figure 10.1 Game-changing innovations: transforming what is possible, redesigning markets in your own vision

requires us. Using technologies such as social networks to plot sightings of species across the world, building up a living picture of life on Planet Earth, where it is in danger and where it is thriving. With this knowledge we can take more focused and immediate action to prevent permanent damage.

2. **The limitless energy grid**

The sun, wind, oceans and subatomic structures have the potential to provide us with unlimited sources of energy. Just as the internet became an open-sourced, distributed network freely available to everyone, so could the future power grids. No longer does the value need to be in extraction and supply, but instead in the way people use it. Pacific Gas & Electric, for example, is currently exploring how they could turn such a game-changing vision into reality. As with most energy companies, it has ventures in solar, wind and wave power, but also in more intriguing areas such as cow energy – turning the huge amounts of methane produced by cattle into electricity. Similarly, if your own solar panels, or cows, produce more energy than you need, you can contribute it to the grid. The 'smart' grid can then harness Web 2.0-like properties to interact with people, enabling them to give and take, track and optimize their energy usage.

3. **Driving on air**

The neighbours have the top brands, the latest models, the go-faster stripes. But what could be cooler than a hydrogen car parked in your driveway? You fill up at the local H_2 station, similar to a vending machine and powered by its own solar panels. You can travel about 100 miles before returning for more without emitting a single molecule of carbon.

It's great for urban driving – getting to work, delivering goods or just looking good. Your local station doesn't need to be part of a huge network, and can be much more convenient than those dirty old petrol stations. The H$_2$ station costs around \$500 to construct, based on an electrolyser, a reverse fuel cell. The electricity separates collected rainwater into hydrogen and oxygen. The hydrogen is compressed and stored, ready for use in a fuel-cell car or an electric/hydrogen hybrid. You could even buy one for yourself. Now that would really turn the neighbours' heads.

4. **Nuclear power for good**

Nuclear energy is popular at last, the clean solution to global warming. The biggest obstacle was not only the fear of leakage and misuse but what to do with the radioactive waste that remains hot and dangerous for thousands of years. Conventional reprocessing left behind a worrying by-product, namely weapons-grade plutonium. But a new recycling technology known as Urex+ extracts reusable uranium and cesium, reducing the waste by 75 per cent. This approach leaves the plutonium useless to terrorists and rogue regimes. New types of nuclear reactors will also be able to burn the reprocessed waste as fuel.

5. **Cleaning up the world**

Over a billion people cannot access clean water. A new solution involves bouncing ultrasound waves through contaminated water, zapping the contaminants. Sound could be a much cheaper alternative to the current techniques of filters and chemicals. Similar approaches have already been used in sanitation systems. Now the probes that produce the sound waves are getting more powerful. Portable 'sonolysis' machines can be deployed easily to remote villages, requiring only sunshine for their power. The same technology could be used to decontaminate polluted water from industry, cleaning up rivers and lakes that currently threaten lives.

Trends in sustainable innovation

Reinier Evers is an open-minded, sustainability-thinking futurist who runs a trend business called trendwatching.com. Rather than imagining what technologies could do in the future, he observes what's actually happening. His challenge is to make sense of the patterns and interpret them as directional trends that are reshaping markets and brands.

He sees five big trends in social and environmental innovation, giving them simple labels to try and make sense of this evolving world:

- **eco-ugly**: products and services that are more sustainable versions of the 'real thing' but don't match up in price, style or performance;

- **eco-embedded**: products and services that embrace sustainability within their design and function but don't make a fuss about it;
- **eco-chic**: products and services that are sustainable and actually look as nice and cool as the less sustainable originals;
- **eco-iconic**: bold designs for products and services that show off their environmental credentials, enabling people to make a statement;
- **eco-boosters**: products and services that go beyond neutralizing their damage, and actually make a positive contribution to the world.

Here are just a small selection picked out by Trendwatching's network of 5,000 trend spotters all round the world looking for emergent behaviours – new products and services, new ways in which people are using them:

1. **Aesthetic ethics**
   Daub & Bauble hand wash, hand lotion and dish detergent come in three scents: Sorrento Lemon & Ginger, Mission Fig & Thyme, and Tarocco Orange & Clove. Packaging features limited-edition patterns designed by Wink (of Target, Macy's, American Eagle Outfitters and The Limited fame, amongst others). Daub & Bauble products use only natural ingredients and the bottles are fully recyclable. Prices: between $8 and $10. Tagline: 'Aesthetics with ethics'. (http://www.daubandbauble.com/)

2. **Bag power**
   Made of Bavarian leather, Noon Solar's Cortland solar-powered bag incorporates a flexible solar panel into the body of each bag, which allows for charging a cellphone or iPod. Collecting energy with the bag is simple. The bag can be placed in a window with the panel facing towards the sun at work, home, at a café, or while walking/biking around town. Even on cloudy or rainy days, energy is collected through the UV light of the sun. The battery pack has a green indicator that lights up when it's charging. (http://www.noonsolar.com/fall-collection/cortland)

3. **Car cleaning**
   BMW's Hydrogen 7 series may not seem very different. Looking exactly like the original, 'dirty' 7 series, it does apparently sport an engine that actively cleans the air, actually showing emissions that, for certain components, such as non-methane organic gases (NMOGs) and carbon monoxides (COs), are cleaner than the ambient air that comes into the car's engine. (http://www.bmwusa.com/Standard/Content/Uniquely/FutureTechnologies/Hydrogen.aspx)

4. **Carbon cards**

   Brazilian Ipiranga gas stations have launched a Carbono Zero credit card in cooperation with MasterCard, which offsets the carbon emissions from their customers. When a customer uses the card to pay for fuel, Ipiranga calculates how much CO_2 emission that amount of fuel represents and will pass part of the sales value to CO_2-neutralization programmes. Means of offsetting CO_2 include reforestation projects, preservation of the rainforest and sponsorship of renewable energy companies. (http://www.cartaocarbonozero.com.br/)

5. **Cargo bikes**

   French company La Petite Reine maintains a fleet of about 60 Cargocycles for hire by businesses that need to make small- to medium-sized urban deliveries over a distance of up to 30 kilometres. Weighing only 80 kg (as opposed to 1,000 kg or more for most delivery vans), each Cargocycle can transport about 180 kg of merchandise in its 1,400-litre cargo space, with the help of an electric assist motor. Cargocycle deliveries are faster than those made via traditional truck, and also 10 to 20 per cent less expensive, La Petite Reine says. It makes some 2,500 less-polluting deliveries every day for clients including DHL, ColiPoste and Monoprix. (http://www.lapetitereine.com/)

6. **Earth points**

   By using GE's Earth Rewards credit card, consumers ensure that a portion of their net expenditure will go to offsetting the emissions created by their purchases and activities. For example, spending $25 contributes enough to offset the emissions associated with running a typical refrigerator for a month. Spending $500 offsets the emissions from driving almost 1,500 miles in an average car. (http://myearthrewards.com/credit card.html?ProspectID=)

7. **Electric speed**

   First unveiled as a prototype in July 2006, Tesla Motors' electric sports car, the Tesla Roadster, is now in regular production. It goes from 0 to 60 mph in just 3.9 seconds, has a top speed of 125 mph (201 km/h) (limited for safety) and has a base price of $98,000. There are already plans to introduce a sedan, competing with the likes of the BMW 5 Series and the Audi A6. (http://www.teslamotors.com/)

8. **Energy rental**

   Citizenré REnU allow consumers to rent a solar-energy system (the REnU) for 1, 5 or 25 years, instead of having to make significant investments by buying one, and having to deal with maintenance. At the end of each month, Citizenré will send a bill showing how much electricity the REnU system has generated that month. The company claims to have signed up over 30,000 people who are interested in participating. (http://renu.citizenre.com)

9. **Kiwi cleaning**

New Zealand-based Beauty Engineered Forever produces a range of environmentally friendly household cleaning products from natural ingredients and essential oils that are not harmful to the environment and safe for consumers. The packaging has been designed to connect with the customer on a personal level with playful and cheeky pick-up lines, such as 'I'll do your dirty work' and 'I'll make it all white.' And yes, it's different enough to be easily recognizable to visitors of one's kitchen. (http://www.bee.net.nz/)

10. **Paper garden**

US-based company Of The Earth sells handmade flower-seed paper that produces a bloom of flowers after being used. The paper sheets can be planted directly into the soil in a pot or in the garden. A fun advertising application of this cradle-to-cradle thinking: when Honda UK wanted to remind avid gardeners that their range of products is not only good for their garden but also good for the environment, they worked with Inferno (http://www.inferno-group.com/) to print the mailer on similar paper containing seeds that could be planted to grow flowers. We know, we know, it's a bit frilly, and a digital mailer would still have been better, but it's the thought (and direction) that counts. (http://www.flowerseedpaper.com/)

11. **Rotating driver**

The Nissan Pivo is a concept car powered by a lithium-ion battery. The car is essentially a 360-degree rotating cabin on a chassis of four wheels, and hence eliminates the need for reversing and makes parking easier. The car's futuristic design incorporates large doors for easy access to the cabin, and large windscreens and windows for high visibility. (http://www.nissan-global.com/EN/PIVO2)

12. **Solar sailing**

Australian company Solar Sailor has developed a 'solar wing' for ferries or yachts, which harvests both sun and wind energy. Like a large sail, the (very iconic) solar wing can be manipulated into different rotating positions, as well as folding flat in high winds. The vessels can reach speeds of 10 to 13 knots, the same maximum speed as conventional ferries. Even on a cloudy day, enough energy is generated to charge the vessel's main batteries and keep the boat running. Solar Sailor-powered vessels are already in service in Sydney Harbour. (http://www.solarsailor.com/)

13. **Sun worshipping**

The Solstice on the Park, a 26-storey residential tower in Chicago's Hyde Park neighbourhood, to be completed by September 2010, is literally shaped by solar access. Its surface is designed at precisely the optimum angle for 41.5 degrees north (Chicago), which allows the sun to enter the apartments during winter for passive solar warming and keeps it out during the summer to reduce air-conditioning use. The sawtooth design creates balconies that block direct midday sun, decreasing the need for power-hungry air conditioning. In winter, when the sun is lower, rays pass through the windows to warm the interior. (http://www.dynamicarchitecture.net/)

14. **Windy tower**

The Bahrain World Trade Center is the world's first commercial building to incorporate large-scale wind turbines into its initial design. It has three massive wind turbines that measure 29 metres in diameter and are supported on bridges between the BWTC's two 240-metre-high towers. The turbines generate approximately 11–15 per cent of the BWTC's total energy needs. (http://www.bahrainwtc.com/)

The list is endless. Around the world, the patterns are emerging. People are embracing a more sustainable world. Business is the catalyst and conduit. Innovation is the key to engaging people in a better, healthier and happier lifestyle.

Business as a force for positive change

Writing a foreword to the great book, *World Changing*, Nobel Prize-winning former US vice president Al Gore writes:

> We find ourselves in a crisis of great magnitude. Mankind is literally changing the balance between people and the atmosphere, leading to an unprecedented warming of the earth.
>
> Despite the wonderful technological advances of the 20th century, we still generate power and fuel our vehicles with coal, oil and gas – and the combustion of those fuels is what is heating up the planet.
>
> Meanwhile more than a billion people find themselves still trapped in dire poverty, hoping for just a percentage of the wealth that we have in the developed world. Millions of children still die from preventable diseases and malnutrition, and throughout much of the world, violence, corruption, terrorism, and oppression are still too frequently the realities of daily life.

Each of these problems is serious. Together they add up to signs that this is a turning point in human civilization, one that requires great moral leadership and generational responsibility. We have a great challenge. However, because we understand the root causes of these problems, we can also join together to solve them.

We need a new vision of the future. The Bible says, 'Where there is no vision, the people perish.' Today, facing so many problems, many of us find it very difficult to envision a better future, much less the kind of solutions that might make such a future possible.

There are many solutions, some little known but well proven, some innovative and new, some bold and yet untried. Taken together, these solutions present a picture of a future that is not dark or catastrophic, but one that is full of hope and within our grasp.

To build that future we need a generation of everyday heroes, people who – whatever their walks of life – have the courage to think in fresh ways and to act to meet this planetary crisis head-on.

Indeed, each one of us can make a difference.

But together we can do so much more. Together we have the capabilities and courage to make an extraordinary impact.

Yet business is probably the only organizing force on the planet that has the structures and incentives to achieve this. Through brands and innovation, business fundamentally changes attitudes and behaviours, forces that can be harnessed to improve ourselves, but also to improve our society and environment.

Whilst business has been much maligned for its negative impacts and its narrow obsession with money, it is now time for business to be a positive force. It is, after all, the enabler of most of our incomes, of most of our consumption, of most of our lives.

It is possible for a business to grow profitably and make a positive difference to people and nature at the same time, and indeed usefully. Doing good is probably the best way to sustain profitable growth.

'People and planet and profit' is not about sustainability in itself, nor should your first step be to develop a sustainability strategy for your business.

It is about business done better, embracing more thoughtful and connected approaches to everything you do. It helps to clarify where you are going, attract more investment, develop more innovative solutions, operate more efficiently, deliver more distinctive products and services, attract the best talent to a more rewarding place to work.

And it gives people a reason to love you again.

Business with a more enlightened purpose, with more inspired leadership and a commitment to growing in new ways really can improve people's lives, and make the world a better place.

Together we can create a new business world.

Part 4

Resources

'Times of turbulence are the most exciting, because they provide the greatest challenges and opportunities,' said Pablo Picasso.

The *People, Planet, Profit* A to Z

From authenticity to zero emissions, the world of sustainability is full of jargon and specialist terms. So is this the vocabulary we need to adopt in the changing business world?

Authenticity Being genuine, natural and honest in your practices. Businesses have become incredibly transparent, as online information is freely available to all, and anybody can access most data about an organization's social and environmental behaviours.

Biodegradable Product has the ability to break down, safely and relatively quickly, by biological means, into the raw materials of nature and are broken down by other living organisms.

Biodiesel Diesel fuel manufactured from vegetable matter rather than non-renewable fossil fuels. It is a variety of biofuel (see below).

Biodiversity In popular usage, this is often used to describe all the species living in a particular area. If we consider this area at its largest scale – the entire world – then biodiversity can be summarized as life on Earth.

Biofuel Fuel derived from renewable raw materials, such as bark, black liquor or logging residuals.

Bottom of the pyramid A term coined by author C K Prahalad to reflect the incredibly large proportion of the world's population that live in or close to poverty. In particular, he describes the tremendous opportunity as these people become more affluent, mobile and ambitious.

Carbon credit Carbon credits (or 'offsets') are created when an emitter of greenhouse gas emissions (ie carbon dioxide, CO_2) makes permanent emissions reductions. For instance, if a large industrial building replaces older, less energy-efficient furnaces with newer, more efficient equipment, they reduce their energy consumption and associated carbon emissions over time. If these greenhouse gas emissions that have been reduced can be quantified or measured, a 'carbon credit' is created and can be sold. The market-trading mechanism for carbon credits is a key programme in the Kyoto Protocol.

Carbon dioxide A colourless, odourless gas that naturally exists in the Earth's atmosphere. As the most prevalent greenhouse gas, CO_2 is known to contribute to global warming and climate change. Atmospheric concentrations of CO_2 have been increasing at a rate of about 0.5 per cent per year and are now approximately 30 per cent above pre-industrial levels. The main source of man-made CO_2 emissions is the combustion of fossil fuels.

Carbon footprint A measure of the amount of carbon dioxide emitted as the result of a particular organization or activity, largely through the combustion of fossil fuels. A carbon footprint is often expressed in terms of tonnes of carbon dioxide or tonnes of carbon emitted, usually on an annual basis. CO_2 is known as a 'greenhouse gas' because it absorbs heat from the sun rather than reflecting it away from the planet. Because of this, scientists have linked a high level of it in the atmosphere to global warming. A carbon footprint is often measured in terms of tonnes of CO_2, which is produced by burning gas, coal or oil for heating and petrol in your car, amongst other things. It is possible to 'offset' your carbon footprint by planting trees, which absorb CO_2 from the atmosphere as part of their life cycle and cancel out the carbon we produce. But experts say it is better to cut your carbon emissions rather than offset what you have already produced.

Carbon neutral Describes a scenario in which the net discharge of carbon dioxide into the atmosphere is zero. First, a calculation is made of the total amount of atmospheric CO_2 emissions for which a particular organization is responsible. Then the organization funds projects that remove the equivalent amount of CO_2 from the atmosphere (or prevent emissions that would otherwise have been inevitable) by means of carbon-offsetting schemes. Some believe that the concept of carbon neutrality is an unattainable ideal given the complexity of the carbon cycle, our poor understanding of it, the uncertainties surrounding carbon reduction and sequestration technologies, and the fact that all human activity, including carbon sequestration, produces carbon emissions of its own.

Carbon offset A strategy adopted by some organizations to balance their own carbon dioxide (CO_2) emissions with equivalent reductions elsewhere. In the early days of carbon offsetting, this typically involved planting trees that would absorb an amount of CO_2 equivalent to the organization's own emissions. Doubts over the validity of forestry-based offsetting, however, have prompted the development of alternatives such as the development of cleaner fuels, the installation of renewable power-generation facilities, and the development of new carbon-reduction and -capture technologies, such as hybrid engines and carbon sequestration. The scientific uncertainties surrounding offsetting, combined with arguments over the monetary value of carbon emissions and the lack of regulation in the offsetting market, have prompted some organizations to manage their offsetting projects directly. For example, Virgin Group has pledged to invest all of the profits from its trains and planes businesses – an estimated £2 billion over three years – in a new Virgin-owned venture to develop renewable fuels.

Clean-burning Not to be confused with 'zero emissions', it describes an energy source that leaves minimal contamination, or less contamination than your average petroleum product. Natural gas, for example, is a clean-burning fuel.

Climate change At present the planet is getting hotter, which, according to scientists, is down to the greenhouse effect. They believe humans producing CO_2 are making the atmosphere warmer. Their vision for the future is that if the temperature continues to go up we will see rising sea and river levels and rainfall, causing flooding and much hotter summers that could cause drought.

Climate neutral Net zero production of greenhouse gases (see also Carbon neutral).

Corporate social responsibility (CSR) Describes how companies integrate social, environmental and ethical concerns into the business decision-making process and their interactions with stakeholders on a voluntary basis. However, CSR has tended to be an add-on agenda for business, championed by a specialist team, rather than a core business activity.

Eco-friendly Little or no impact on the native eco-system.

Eco-labelling A method of identifying products that cause less damage to the environment or society than other products (such as fair trade, organic, Food Alliance-certified, raised without antibiotics, FSC, MSC). There exists a wide selection of eco-labels with different criteria and varying degrees of legitimacy. Whilst some labels indicate that the product was produced according to strict guidelines enforced and verified by third-party certifying agencies, other labels are self-awarded by producers.

Ecological footprint The area of land and water needed to produce the resources to entirely sustain a human population and absorb its waste products with prevailing technology. The concept of an ecological footprint is used as a resource-management and community-planning tool.

Ecological footprint analysis The area of land and water that ecosystems require, on a continuous basis, to produce the resources we consume and to assimilate the wastes we produce, wherever on Earth the land/water is located. The global average is 2.2 hectares per person, whereas, for example, it takes 6.4 hectares (16 acres) to support the lifestyle of the average Canadian.

Energy efficiency Ratio of energy output of a conversion process or of a system to its energy input. The use of minimal power, with little or no wastage, to achieve a result. Steel makers are always looking for ways to improve energy efficiency.

Energy from waste A method of harnessing the power released by burning (incinerating) rubbish.

Fair trade The more equitable practice of sourcing from producers in a way that creates a win-win, ensures that they receive a reasonable price for their goods, often doing more to support the development of their businesses, and are not taken advantage of by larger companies. The Fairtrade Foundation seeks to approve the use of the phrase.

Food miles The distance food travels from where it is produced to your plate, and the impact of this on the environment. The further it travels, the more fuel has to be used to transport it and the more CO_2 is produced (see Carbon footprint). To reduce your food miles, try to buy locally produced food.

Food security Access by all people at all times to enough food for an active, healthy life. Food security includes at a minimum ready availability of nutritionally adequate and safe foods and an assured ability to acquire acceptable foods in socially acceptable ways (United States Department of Agriculture).

Footprint A person's, company's or organization's overall impact, usually with reference to its environmental impacts, but sometimes also referring to its economic and social ones.

Fossil fuels Fuels found in the Earth's strata that are derived from the fossilized remains of animal and plant matter over millions of years. Fossil fuels include oil, natural gas and coal. Fossil fuels are considered to be non-renewable because they are consumed faster than they can be produced by natural processes.

Genetically modified (GM) foods GM foods and other types of new foods can only be marketed in the European Union if they have passed a rigorous safety assessment. In the EU, if a food contains or consists of genetically modified organisms (GMOs), or contains ingredients produced from GMOs, this must be indicated on the label.

Genetically modified organism (GMO) This is a plant or animal that has been genetically engineered. Many governments and industries support the use of GMOs, but there is strong opposition from many consumers, NGOs and other opinion formers. It is legal for farmers in the United States and some other countries (eg Argentina) to produce and sell certain GMOs for human and animal consumption. In Europe and Japan, they are banned pending further safety trials.

Global warming An increase in the global mean temperature of the Earth as a result of increased emissions of greenhouse gases (see below). Global warming is believed to have adverse consequences such as climate change and a rise in sea levels. The scientific community is in general agreement that the Earth's surface has warmed by about 1° F in the past 140 years.

Green A term widely used to describe minimal negative impact to the environment. Although it usually refers only to environmental impacts, some commentators now use it also to cover social and ethical impacts.

Greenhouse effect The effect produced as greenhouse gases allow incoming solar radiation to pass through the Earth's atmosphere, but prevent part of the outgoing infrared radiation from the Earth's surface and lower atmosphere from escaping into outer space. This process occurs naturally and has kept the Earth's temperature about 59° F warmer than it would otherwise be. Current life on Earth could not be sustained without the natural greenhouse effect.

Greenhouse gases A collective term for the following gases: carbon dioxide (CO_2), methane (CH4), nitrous oxide (N2O), hydrofluorocarbons (HFCs), perfluorocarbons (PFCs), and sulphur hexafluoride (SF6).

Greenwash Superficial marketing activities that seek to overstate a brand's environmental performance or 'jump on the bandwagon' without significant evidence.

Landfill A method for final disposal of solid waste on land. The refuse is spread and compacted and a cover of soil applied so that effects on the environment (including public health and safety) are minimized. Landfills are required to have liners and leachate treatment systems to prevent contamination of ground water and surface water. An industrial landfill disposes of non-hazardous industrial wastes.

Life cycle assessment (LCA) A method for assessing the environmental impact of a product 'from the cradle to the grave'.

Methane Often an emission of animal waste, this is a greenhouse gas, which means that it contributes to global warming.

Offset See Carbon offset.

Organic In order to be labelled 'organic', a product, its producer, and/or the farmer must meet the organic standards. There are many standards in place and it is important to do some research to find out what's behind the standard. Generally, organic foods cannot be grown using synthetic fertilizers, chemicals or sewage sludge, cannot be genetically modified, and cannot be irradiated. Organic meat and poultry are usually fed only organically grown feed (without any animal by-products) and often cannot be treated with hormones or antibiotics. Many standards also require that animals must have access to the outdoors, and ruminants must have access to pasture.

Ozone (O3) An important greenhouse gas found in both the stratosphere and the troposphere. In the stratosphere, ozone provides a protective layer shielding the Earth from ultraviolet radiation and consequent harmful health effects on humans and the environment. In the troposphere (including at ground level), oxygen molecules in ozone combine with other chemicals and gases (oxidization) to cause smog.

Ozone depletion Stratospheric ozone is necessary to filter out harmful radiation from the sun. Scientists have linked depletion of stratospheric ozone to increased incidence of skin cancer and other disorders and environmental degradation. Under international conventions and national laws, governments are prohibiting the production, use and release of ozone-depleting substances.

Ozone layer The protective layer in the Earth's upper atmosphere, which absorbs some of the sun's ultraviolet rays, thereby reducing the amount of potentially harmful radiation that reaches the Earth's surface.

Recycling The process by which materials are collected and used as 'raw' materials for new products. There are three steps in recycling: materials are source-separated and collected; materials are processed and manufactured into new products; consumers purchase the goods made with reprocessed materials.

Reuse To find a new function for an item that has outgrown its original use; to use it again (eg peanut-butter jar for a collection; washing and reusing dishes).

Stewardship Caring for land and resources with the intent to pass on healthy ecosystems to future generations.

Sustainability The concept that new development must meet the needs of the present without compromising those of the future. Sustainability is measured in three interdependent dimensions that are sometimes collectively referred to as the triple bottom line (see below): the society, the environment, and economically – sometimes referred to as people, planet and profit.

Sustainable development Development that meets the needs of present generations without compromising the ability of future generations to meet their own needs (United Nations).

Triple bottom line The economic, social and environmental performance of an organization or project. This concept extends the principles of classic accountancy to the measurement and reporting of environmental and social performance.

Waste stream This describes the channelling of household rubbish into a system for processing. The waste stream begins at the domestic dustbin and ends with recycling or landfill.

Waste-treatment plant This is the place where household rubbish is processed and prepared for recycling, for incineration or for disposal in landfill sites.

Zero emissions Often used to describe a net carbon emission of zero; however, should also include other types of emissions, and ideally no emissions at all but rather a net balance.

The *People, Planet, Profit* blueprint

How good are you, how good do you need to be? What matters most?

This simple diagnostic is based on the three sustainable 'growth wheels', evaluating how well you approach each and how well you integrate the three wheels together.

It provides a starting point for understanding how advanced your organization is in each of the different areas, and how good you need to be – given your type of business, your market and your ambitions. This gap analysis can then be used to prioritize and balance future initiatives, and illustrates how sustainable practices must integrate economically.

These audits are just a starting point. An integrated business strategy that embraces the opportunities of sustainability at its core, and brings together the many different priorities for action, is then developed.

A more detailed diagnostic process is available from www.Peopleand PlanetandProfit.com.

The *People, Planet, Profit* directory

How do you find the help you need as you set out on the journey to sustainable success? In addition to the specialist resources described below, there are many other organizations and websites providing information, resources and specialist services:

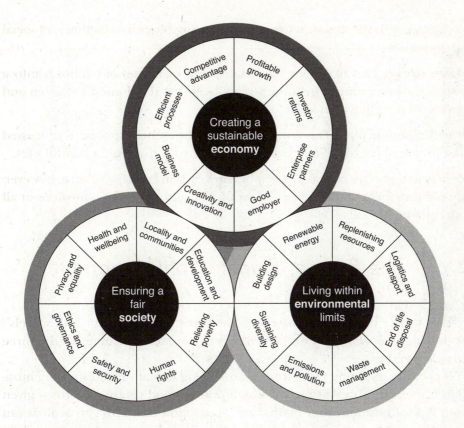

Figure iv.1   People and planet and profit: evaluating your business based on existing and desired performance on each of the factors, within each of the three 'growth wheels'

- Ashoka, a community of social entrepreneurs: www.ashoka.org
- Business for Social Responsibility: global advice network: www.bsr.org
- Business in the Community: helping you to do more: www.bitc.org.uk
- Carbon footprint: calculate your impact and more: www.carbonfootprint. com
- Carbon Trust: helping business to cut emissions: www.carbontrust.co.uk
- Centre for Sustainable Design: design and innovation: www.cfsd.org.uk
- Climate Group: seeking a low-carbon economy: www.climategroup.org. uk
- CSR Europe: one of the best CSR toolboxes: www.csreurope.org
- Dow Jones Sustainability Index: www.sustainability-index.com

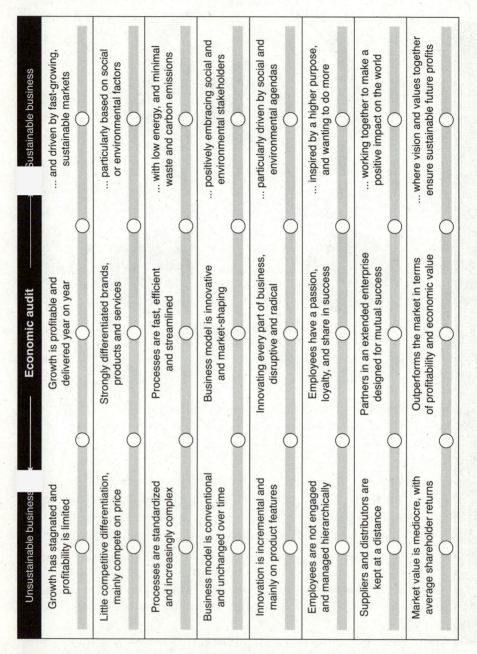

Unsustainable business		Economic audit		Sustainable business
Growth has stagnated and profitability is limited		Growth is profitable and delivered year on year		… and driven by fast-growing, sustainable markets
Little competitive differentiation, mainly compete on price		Strongly differentiated brands, products and services		… particularly based on social or environmental factors
Processes are standardized and increasingly complex		Processes are fast, efficient and streamlined		… with low energy, and minimal waste and carbon emissions
Business model is conventional and unchanged over time		Business model is innovative and market-shaping		… positively embracing social and environmental stakeholders
Innovation is incremental and mainly on product features		Innovating every part of business, disruptive and radical		… particularly driven by social and environmental agendas
Employees are not engaged and managed hierarchically		Employees have a passion, loyalty, and share in success		… inspired by a higher purpose, and wanting to do more
Suppliers and distributors are kept at a distance		Partners in an extended enterprise designed for mutual success		… working together to make a positive impact on the world
Market value is mediocre, with average shareholder returns		Outperforms the market in terms of profitability and economic value		… where vision and values together ensure sustainable future profits

Figure iv.2 The economic blueprint: where are you now, where do you want to be, and where are the priorities to deliver good growth?

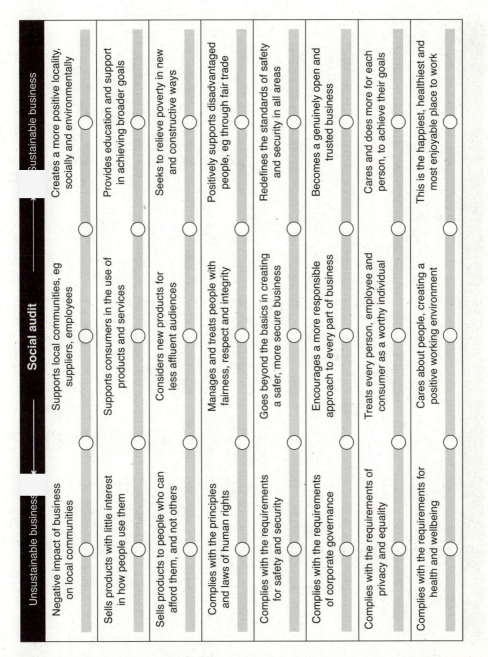

Figure iv.3 The social blueprint: where are you now, where do you want to be, and where are the priorities to deliver good growth?

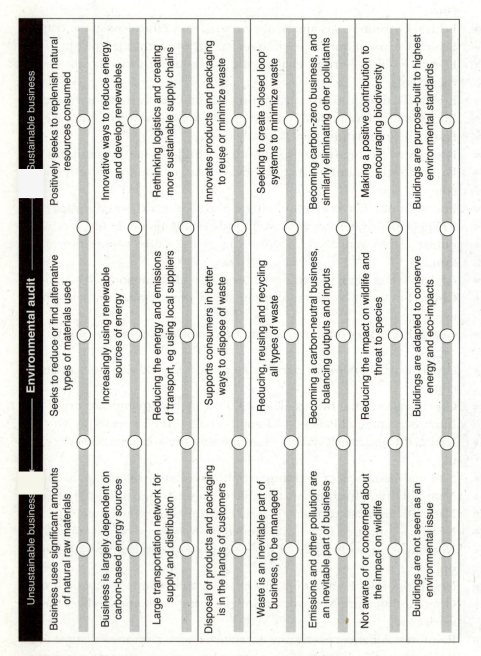

Unsustainable business	Environmental audit		Sustainable business
Business uses significant amounts of natural raw materials	Seeks to reduce or find alternative types of materials used		Positively seeks to replenish natural resources consumed
Business is largely dependent on carbon-based energy sources	Increasingly using renewable sources of energy		Innovative ways to reduce energy and develop renewables
Large transportation network for supply and distribution	Reducing the energy and emissions of transport, eg using local suppliers		Rethinking logistics and creating more sustainable supply chains
Disposal of products and packaging is in the hands of customers	Supports consumers in better ways to dispose of waste		Innovates products and packaging to reuse or minimize waste
Waste is an inevitable part of business, to be managed	Reducing, reusing and recycling all types of waste		Seeking to create 'closed loop' systems to minimize waste
Emissions and other pollution are an inevitable part of business	Becoming a carbon-neutral business, balancing outputs and inputs		Becoming carbon-zero business, and similarly eliminating other pollutants
Not aware of or concerned about the impact on wildlife	Reducing the impact on wildlife and threat to species		Making a positive contribution to encouraging biodiversity
Buildings are not seen as an environmental issue	Buildings are adapted to conserve energy and eco-impacts		Buildings are purpose-built to highest environmental standards

Figure iv.4 The environmental blueprint: where are you now, where do you want to be, and where are the priorities to deliver good growth?

- Environmental Leader: news and research: www.environmentalleader.com
- Ethical Consumer: sustainability research: www.ethicalconsumer.com
- Ethical Corporation: the leading magazine: www.ethicalcorp.com
- Ethical Fashion Forum: challenging an industry: www.ethicalfashionforum.com
- Ethical Trading Initiative: promoting ethical trade: www.ethicaltrade.org
- European Environmental Agency: part of the EU: www.eea.europa.eu
- Fairtrade Foundation: www.fairtrade.org.uk
- Forest Stewardship Council: supporting world forests: wwwfscus.org
- Forum for the Future: sustainable development: www.forumforthefuture.com
- Friends of the Earth: championing a healthier world: www.foe.org
- FTSE 4 Good Index: www.ftse.com/indices/ftse4good_index_series
- Future Exploration Network: the big global shifts: www.futureexploration.net
- Global Action Plan: practical solutions: www.globalactionplan.org.uk
- Global Footprint Network: a sustainability think tank: www.footprintnetwork.org
- Global Reporting Initiative: setting new standards: www.globalreporting.org
- Greenbiz: daily news on sustainable business worldwide: www.greenbiz.com
- Greenpeace: giving the fragile earth a voice: www.greenpeace.org
- Intergovernmental Panel on Climate Change (IPCC): www.ipcc.ch
- National Consumer Council: championing the consumer: www.ncc.org.uk
- National Geographic: inspiring people: www.nationalgeographic.com
- Natural Capital Institute: sustainable research: www.naturalcapital.org
- Nature Conservancy: protecting the environment: www.nature.org
- NESTA: supporting more enlightened innovation: www.nesta.org.uk
- Net Impact: encouraging business leaders to change: www.netimpact.org
- New Economics Foundation: business research: www.neweconomics.org
- Open Architecture Network: improving living: www.openarchitecturenetwork.com
- Rainforest Alliance: protecting ecosystems: www.rainforest-alliance.org
- Rocky Mountain Institute: using natural resources better: www.rmi.org
- Social Accountability International: standards body: www.sa-intl.org
- Social Enterprise Coalition: business and society: www.socialenterprise.org.uk

- SustainAbility: the independent think tank : www.sustainability.com
- Sustainable Development Commission: www.sd-commission.org.uk
- Tomorrow's Company: a new vision of business : www.tomorrowscompany.com
- Transparency International: fighting against corruption: www.transparency.org
- Treehugger: sustainable designs: news and research: www.treehugger.com
- Trendwatching: exploring what happens next: www.trendwatching:com
- UN Environmental Programme: information and education: www.unep.org
- World Business Council for Sustainable Development : www.wbcsd.org
- World Changing: ideas and tools for a better future: www.worldchanging.com
- World Economic Forum: politics and business: www.weforum.com
- World Resources Institute: seeking to reduce climate change: www.wri.org
- Worldwide Fund for Nature (WWF): people and nature: www.wwf.org

More details, links and downloads are available at www.PeopleandPlanetandProfit.com

The *People, Planet, Profit* programme

How can you get your team to explore the ideas in *People, Planet, Profit* and what they mean for your business? Where do you start in applying these approaches in relevant ways for you? How do you get your people to start thinking and acting differently?

The PPP programme is an accelerated development experience for senior and middle managers. It can be tailored to the specific issues in your business, and can be delivered as a learning experience or as a practical way to start addressing your real issues.

The PPP programme is typically delivered as an executive retreat – a four-day accelerated learning experience, when we will also explore the more personal challenges of leadership.

Day 1, pm: World changing

- Making sense of the changing business world;
- Global challenges, shifting power, instant and connected;

- Balancing economic, social and environmental agendas;
- Best practices: from Air Asia and Amazon to Zara and Zopa;
- Essential tools: future radar, scenario planning, customer insight.

Day 2, am: Inspiring purpose

- The enlightened business, one with a purpose beyond profits;
- How business can make a bigger difference to our worlds;
- Aligning a higher purpose with the pursuit of value creation;
- Best practices: from Camper and Cemex to Danone and Disney;
- Essential tools: purpose definition, corporate brands, storytelling.

Day 2, pm: Growth strategy

- Making better strategic choices in times of change;
- Choosing the best markets, better differentiation and business models;
- Aligning the organization to work within strategic rules;
- Best practices: GE gets imagination whilst Tata focuses on new markets;
- Essential tools: value disciplines, strategy framework, GG planning.

Day 3, am: Authentic leadership

- Management and leadership, heads up or heads down;
- Why business needs new leaders for a new world;
- Inspiring direction, disciplined decisions, building teams;
- Best practices: Apple beyond Jobs; Rosso and the engine of Diesel;
- Essential tools: 5C leadership model, personal effectiveness framework.

Day 3, pm: Sustainable innovation

- Creative disruption and renewal, innovation and entrepreneurship;
- Future-back thinking, outside in action, left- and right-brain people;
- Ventures, incubators and rocket ships for practical innovation;
- Best practices: LEGO's creative play and GE's sustainable creativity;
- Essential tools: creative disruption, sustainable business models.

Day 4, am: Personal well-being

- Living, loving and thriving in the new business world;
- Health and fitness; how to feel good and how to do more;
- Confidence and courage; how to stretch and surprise yourself;
- Best practices: from Google's work style to Virgin's lifestyle;
- Essential tools: body works, mind works, action works.

Day 4, pm: Enlightened performance

- Delivering results, short and long term, in crisis and in good times;
- Value creation, value drivers and value management;
- Metrics and scorecards, incentives and rewards;
- Best practices: Toyota's performance culture, Nokia's contrasting approach;
- Essential tools: performance metrics, rewards, value management.

Day 5, am: Real commitment

- What it takes to become a new business leader;
- Planning the change programme for you and your business;
- Milestones and work streams; how to make change happen;
- Best practices: Nike Considered and Unilever's holistic approach;
- Essential tools: impact zoning, leader guide, 90-day plans.

The PPP programme is also delivered as a series of three separate issue- and action-focused workshops for small teams of management, based around phases of discovery, design and delivery. This is a more consultative approach, building on the existing progress and priorities, issues and ideas within your business.

A more detailed programme is available from www.PeopleandPlanetand-Profit.com.

Authors and contributors

Peter Fisk

Peter is a bestselling author and inspirational speaker, an advisor to leading companies around the world and an experienced business leader. He was recently described by *Business Strategy Review* as 'one of the best new business thinkers'.

He is founder and CEO of the GeniusWorks (www.theGeniusWorks.com), a strategic innovation business that works with senior management to 'see things differently' – to develop and implement more inspired strategies for customers, innovation and marketing. The Genius Lab is a facilitated innovation process for developing new business and customer strategies based on deep customer insights and creative thinking, Zoom Ventures bring together business investors and social entrepreneurs, and The Fast Track is a coaching and personal development programme that combines leading-edge learning with fast practical solutions for implementation.

Peter is also author of four other books, including the bestselling *Marketing Genius*, which explores the left- and right-brain approaches to competitive success, and has been translated into more than 28 languages. *Customer Genius* provokes you to rethink how to do business – from the outside in – seeing things differently, and then working on their terms. *The Complete CEO*, with Mark Thomas and Gary Miles, defines a new blueprint for business leadership, and *Business Genius* describes how to create a more inspired approach to business, from the future back and now forward, converting radical ideas into practical, profitable actions.

Peter grew up in the remote farming community of Northumberland, in the north-east of England, and after exploring the world of nuclear physics joined British Airways at a time when it was embarking upon becoming 'the world's favourite airline' with a cultural alignment around customers. He is married with two young daughters and lives in London, England.

He was the transforming CEO of the Chartered Institute of Marketing, the world's largest marketing organization. He led the strategic marketing consulting team of PA Consulting Group, was managing director of specialist measurement firm Brand Finance, and partner of the innovation specialists, The Foundation.

He has worked with companies large and small, across sectors and around the world. His clients include American Express and Coca-Cola, Co-operative Bank, Lastminute.com, Marks & Spencer, Microsoft, O2, Orange, Red Bull, Shell, Turkcell, Virgin, Vodafone and Volkswagen. He encourages leaders to take new perspectives, to learn from new places, to think and act differently, and deliver extraordinary results.

Peter was supported in researching and developing the book by the contributors listed below.

Diana Verde Nieto

Diana is the founder of Clownfish, a sustainability consulting firm, based in London, New York and Shanghai (www.clownfish.co.uk). She brings together 14 years of marketing communications and sustainability experience, putting people and planet at the heart of a business's pursuit of profit, and encouraging commercial organizations to be a force for good.

Clownfish was one of the first consultancies to specialize in sustainability and communications, and now supports many of the world's leading brands and companies including Unilever, Coca-Cola, Reebok, and Timberland. In 2008, Aegis Media acquired a majority stake in the company, and as part of the Isobar network Clownfish can now support 38 markets, combining global vision with local action.

Diana is now predominantly based in Shanghai, applying best practice on sustainability and brand reputation to companies operating in the dynamic and fast-growing Chinese economy.

She also works closely with the WWF, Climate Group, Clinton Global Initiative, and the RSA's Tomorrow's Company.

Anthony Kleanthous

Anthony is senior policy advisor to the WWF in the UK (www.wwf.org.uk) and also a specialist writer and advisor to businesses on sustainable development.

He authored several influential reports on business sustainability, including *Let Them Eat Cake* and *Deeper Luxury* for the WWF, and *Facts and Trends on Sustainable Consumption* for the World Business Council for Sustainable Development. He also supports the UK government's Wellbeing Indicators Group, is a board member of Sustain, and a judge in the International Advertising Association's inaugural Responsibility Awards and the Green Awards.

Anthony's previous career in advertising with Saatchi & Saatchi and then DDB Needham, and in senior marketing roles with AstraZeneca, PayPal and Top Table, enables him to place environmental and social considerations firmly in a commercial framework. He also holds an MSc/DIC with Distinction in Environmental Technology.

Sustainable business leaders who contributed significantly to the book were:

Dan Esty, Yale University

Dan is the Director of the Yale Center for Environmental Law and Policy. He is the author of numerous books and articles on environmental policy issues and the relationships between environment and corporate strategy, competitiveness, trade, globalization, governance and development. His most recent book, *Green to Gold*, argues that pollution control and natural resource management have become critical elements of marketplace success.

Richard Gillies, Marks & Spencer

Richard is the director of Plan A, M&S's integrated approach to sustainability. M&S recently made headlines with its £200-million 'eco-plan' that includes labelling air-freighted food, improving energy efficiency by 25 per cent, and increasing its use of renewable energy. As director of store development at

M&S, Richard is responsible for expanding the company's plan through existing stores, their redevelopment and new concept stores.

Santiago Gowland, Unilever

Santiago is Unilever's global vice president of corporate social responsibility. He works to integrate economic, social and environmental strategies into the organization's business strategy and brand development, seeking a values-led approach to business. He began his career as a lawyer in Argentina, where he started two NGOs, one focusing on handicapped children, the other on micro-finance. He joined the corporate relations team at Unilever in 1999.

Jonathan Horrell, Kraft

Jonathan is Kraft's corporate affairs director, UK and Ireland, and has responsibility for external and internal communications, issues management and community involvement. He joined Kraft in 2003 and has managed communications programmes supporting the company's introduction of coffees from Rainforest Alliance Certified farms to the UK and Ireland, including media relations and stakeholder engagement.

Hannah Jones, Nike

Hannah is Nike's vice president of corporate responsibility, and works closely with CEO Mark Parker in making sustainability a key agenda throughout the sportswear company. She joined Nike in 1998 as director of government and community affairs in EMEA, and now has overall responsibility for managing Nike's global corporate responsibility team, including labour compliance, global community affairs, stakeholder engagement and corporate responsibility strategic planning and business integration.

Harriet Lamb, Fairtrade Foundation

Harriet has been the executive director of the Fairtrade Foundation since 2001. She has guided the Foundation through a period of significant growth, with estimated sales of fair-trade products in the UK increasing from £30 million to £290 million in five years, and more than 3,500 products carrying the Fairtrade mark. In her book, *Fighting the Banana Wars*, she explains that fair trade is a better deal for workers and farmers in the developing world.

Colin le Duc, Generation Investment Management

Colin is the senior portfolio manager for the Generation IM climate solutions strategy. Prior to co-founding Generation, Colin was research director at Sustainable Asset Management in Zurich, Switzerland. At SAM, he ran the analyst team conducting sustainability research on large-capitalization companies globally with the aim of selecting companies for the Dow Jones Sustainability Indexes and SAM's actively managed sustainable investment funds. He has also worked for Arthur D. Little in London as a strategy consultant.

Nigel Morris, Aegis

Nigel is CEO of Isobar, the digital marketing division of Aegis. For almost five years he has been leading the growth, integration and overall strategy of Isobar, which has evolved into the world's largest digital advertising network in 38 countries. In 2005 he was voted one of *Advertising Age*'s Top 10 Global Marketers to Watch, and in 2006 he was listed at number four in *Revolution* magazine's Power 50. Nigel is also a frequent speaker at events such as the World Economic Forum and Cannes advertising festival.

David Nussbaum, WWF

David Nussbaum joined WWF in the UK as chief executive in May 2007. He is also a non-executive director of the quoted private equity fund, Low Carbon Accelerator, and of the leading fair-trade finance company, Shared Interest. Until 2006, he was the (non-executive) chair of Traidcraft, the leading UK fair-trade company. He is also a member of the Council of the RSA.

David Singleton, Arup

David is chairman of Arup's Global Infrastructure Business. He joined Arup in 1973 and is currently a member of the group board and chairman of the Arup Partnerships. He guides the delivery of sustainable solutions valued by clients, communities and end users of Arup's infrastructure services. In addition to his other global responsibilities, David also holds the group board portfolio for corporate sustainability.

Dilys Williams, London College of Fashion

Dilys is the director for sustainable fashion at LCF. She has worked in the fashion industry as a womenswear designer with the likes of Katharine

Hamnett and Stella McCartney for almost 20 years. She is the course director for MA Fashion and the Environment and sits on the steering panels of a number of organizations including Made By, Fashioning an Ethical Industry and the RITE Group.

Thanks

The author would like to thank each contributor for their fabulous insights.

Additionally, thanks to the many others who made this book possible: editor Jon Finch and Helen Savill at Kogan Page, literary agent Simon Benham at MayerBenham, Reinier Evers at Trendwatching, the research team at Green Sky Thinking, Carl Sharples at Co-operative Financial Services, Mark Thomas at PA Consulting Group, and the team of sustainability experts at Clownfish – including Laurence MacSween, Katie Chapman, Becky Willan, Carolin Schramm and Hannah Lane – for all their great support.

More details, links and downloads are available at
www.PeopleandPlanetandProfit.com.

Index

NB: page numbers in *italics* indicates a figure or table

With over 42 years of publishing, more than 80 million people have succeeded in business with thanks to **Kogan Page**

www.koganpage.com

Kogan Page